when the secret hour of pleasure nears

the poetry of T.S. Simmons

with photographs by Cameron MacMaster

iUniverse, Inc.
Bloomington

When the Secret Hour of Pleasure Nears
The Poetry of T.S. Simmons

iUniverse books may be ordered through booksellers or by contacting:

iUniverse
1663 Liberty Drive
Bloomington, IN 47403
www.iuniverse.com
1-800-Authors (1-800-288-4677)

Because of the dynamic nature of the Internet, any web addresses or links contained in this book may have changed since publication and may no longer be valid.

ISBN: 978-1-4620-0976-3 (sc)
ISBN: 978-1-4620-0977-0 (ebk)

Printed in the United States of America

iUniverse rev. date: 6/2/2011

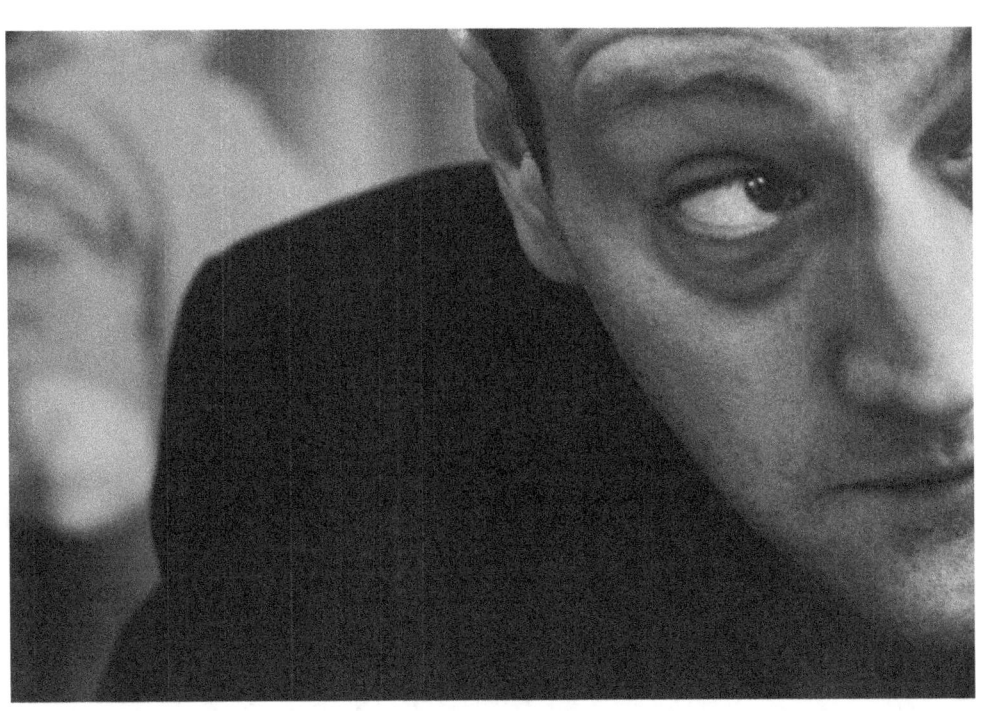

To B,
...the living poem

when the secret hour
of pleasure nears

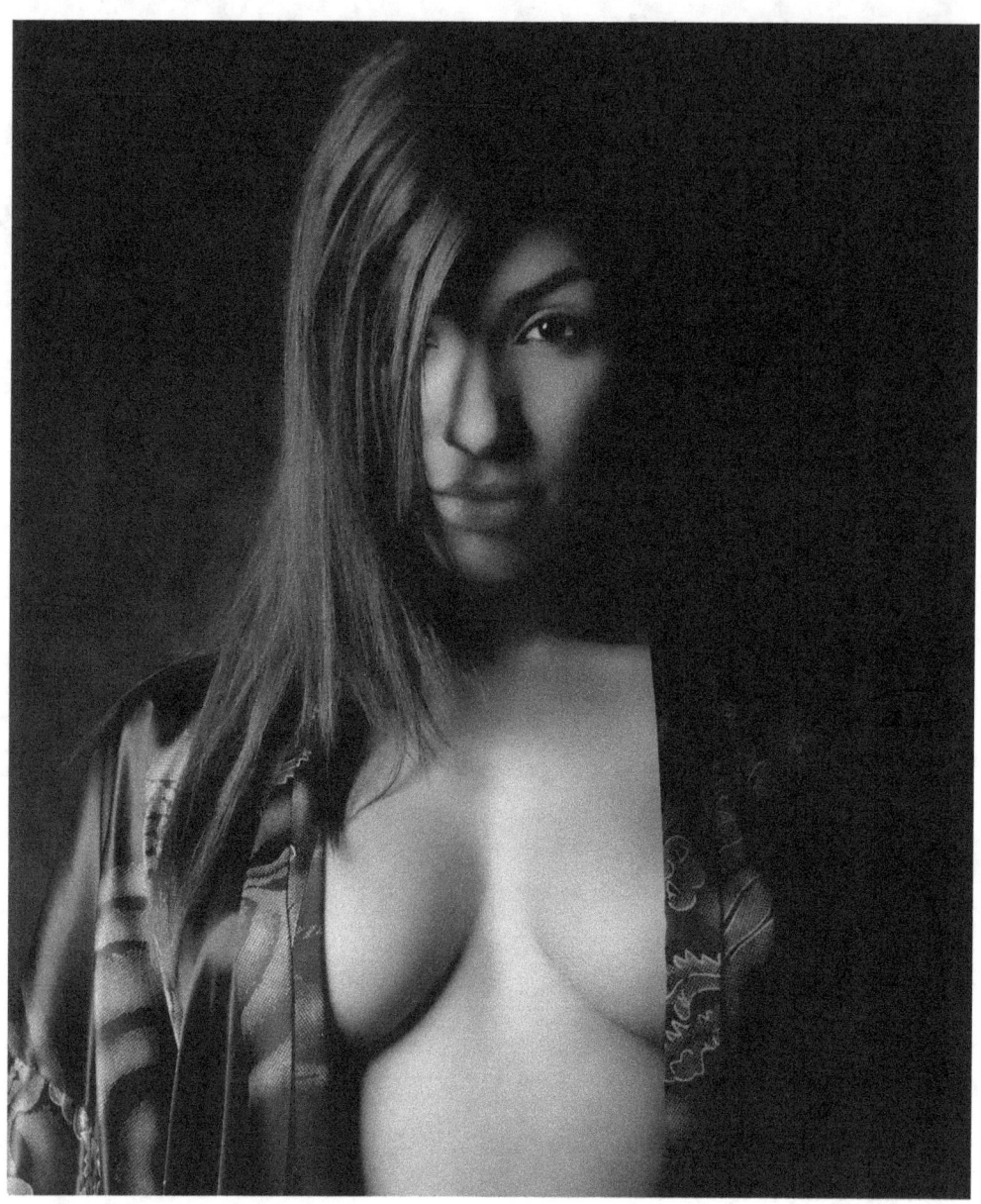

I know
a girl
her eyes
veiled in darkness

not the darkness of Montmartre at night
with warmth reflecting
in the shadows of the boulevards

rather
she resonates
fevered images of sex and death

myself to unearth

if I come home

to discover

her presence

haunting the spaces
beneath the floor, and through the mirrors

I can't even look there
I never could.

Her desire to possess me
Is a violent secrecy

Each of us has his own Infernic visions
tapping vaguely upon the door

I've been choosing to hide
In momentary stupor

From the aching thorns of love.

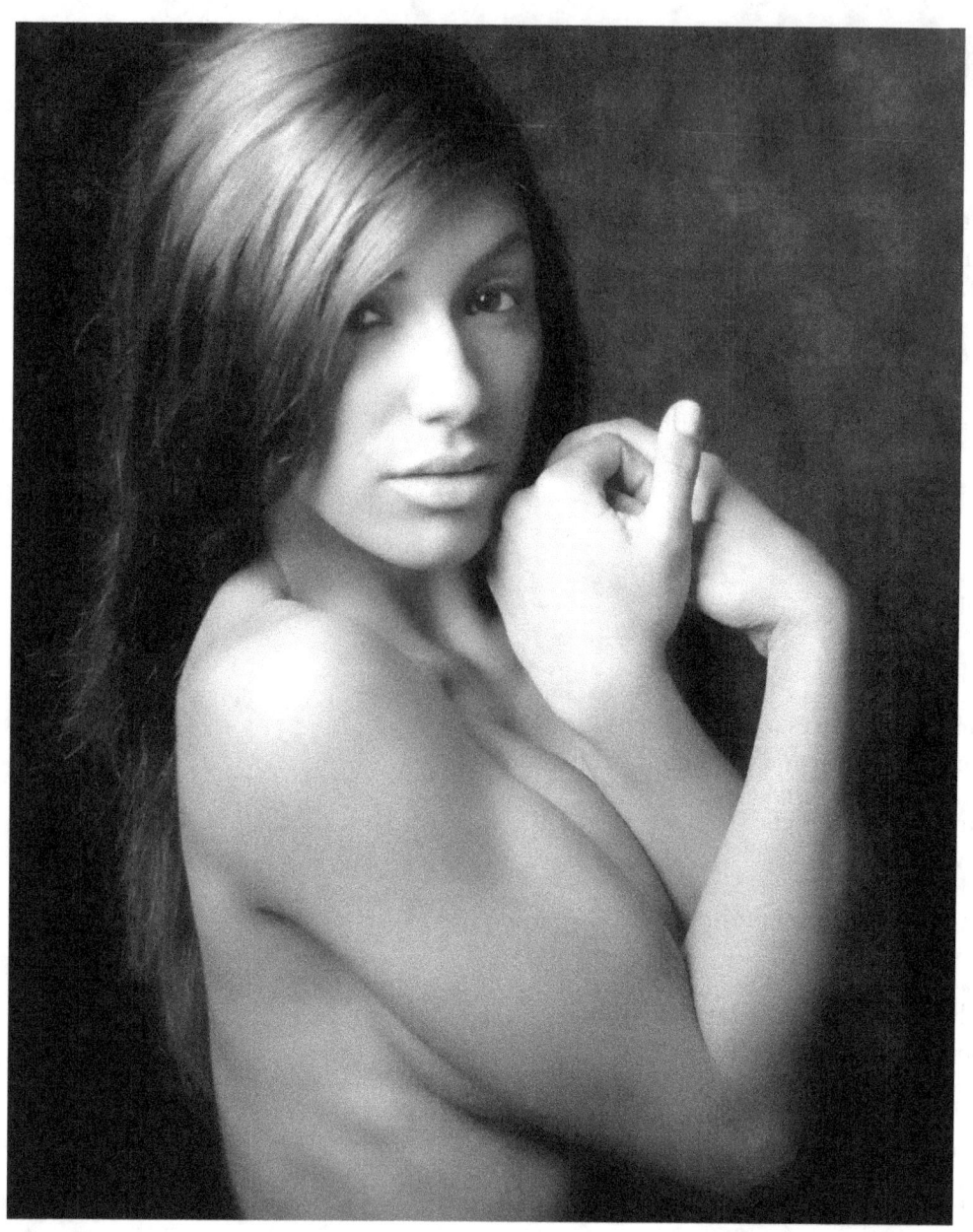

My imagination soars on lonely nights
when the secret hour of pleasure nears
to search within the darkness
for the beauty of your flesh

Your taste intoxicating
and resting upon my swollen lips
which blindly beg in throated whispers
for you to poison me
with
sacred
venom.

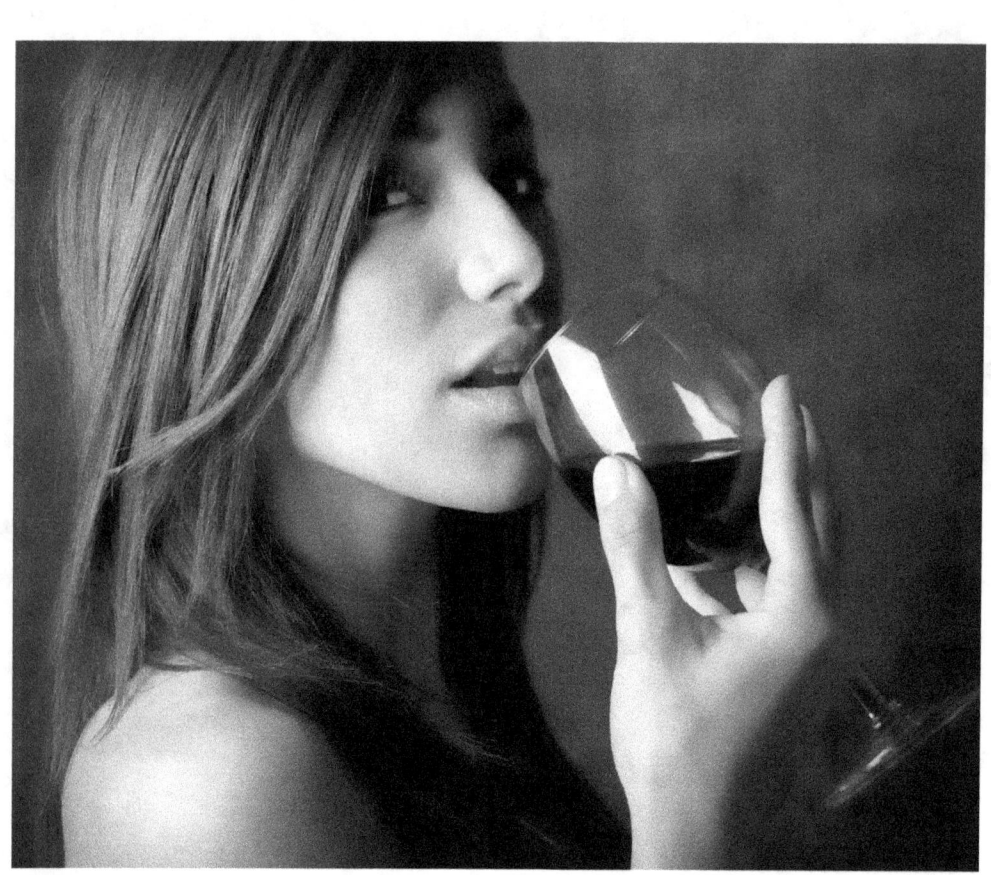

I studied your profile in the shadowed café
As drunkenness afforded me the courage to stare
Upon your rapturous eyes
Stark amongst the fragile paleness
Of your skin
I lit a cigarette to conceal myself
Within the morbid pleasures of night
Though you tinted the spirals of smoke
With enflamed passions
And sadness.
You traced your hair, unconscious
Of the muted tones
Resounding within my deadened ears
I desired to grasp my remorseless heart
And taste the wine burning upon
Your lips

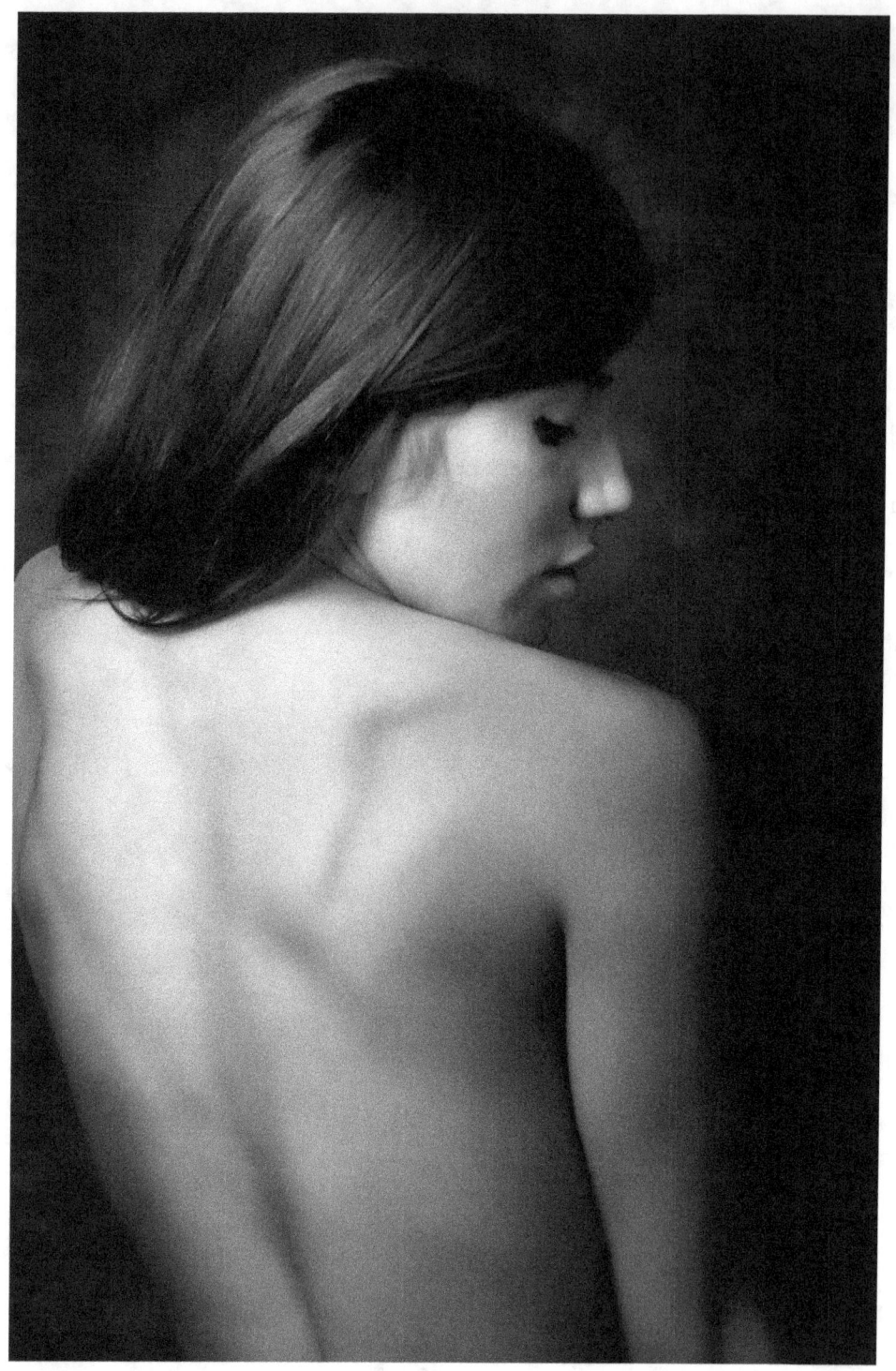

Thank you for your constant and
Ill disguised blessings
They rest upon my skin
And burn translucent
Into the night

I sat in paralysis
Upon the jazz soaked corners
Of my early-morning bed
And smoked while
Thinking of you

You probably didn't even know

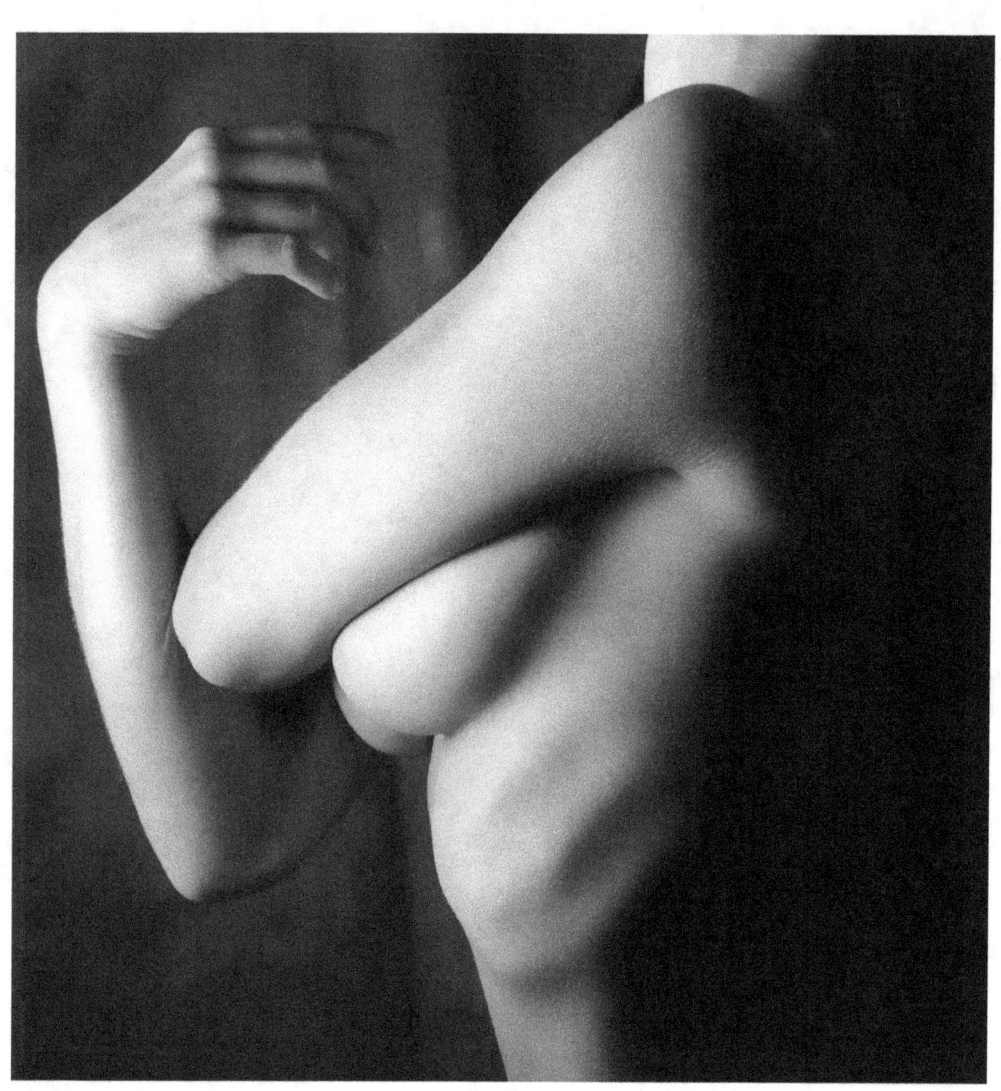

Lady, where have you been
I have a bottle of wine
In your name alone
My lips dry
With longing

I have never believed
In love, nor life
Though I may reconsider
Within your lustful
Presence

Come stand at the window
The soft drapery
Will shroud you against
The icy kiss
Of evening

And I, caressing
The sweet impermanence
Will quietly lament
The exodus of
Beauty

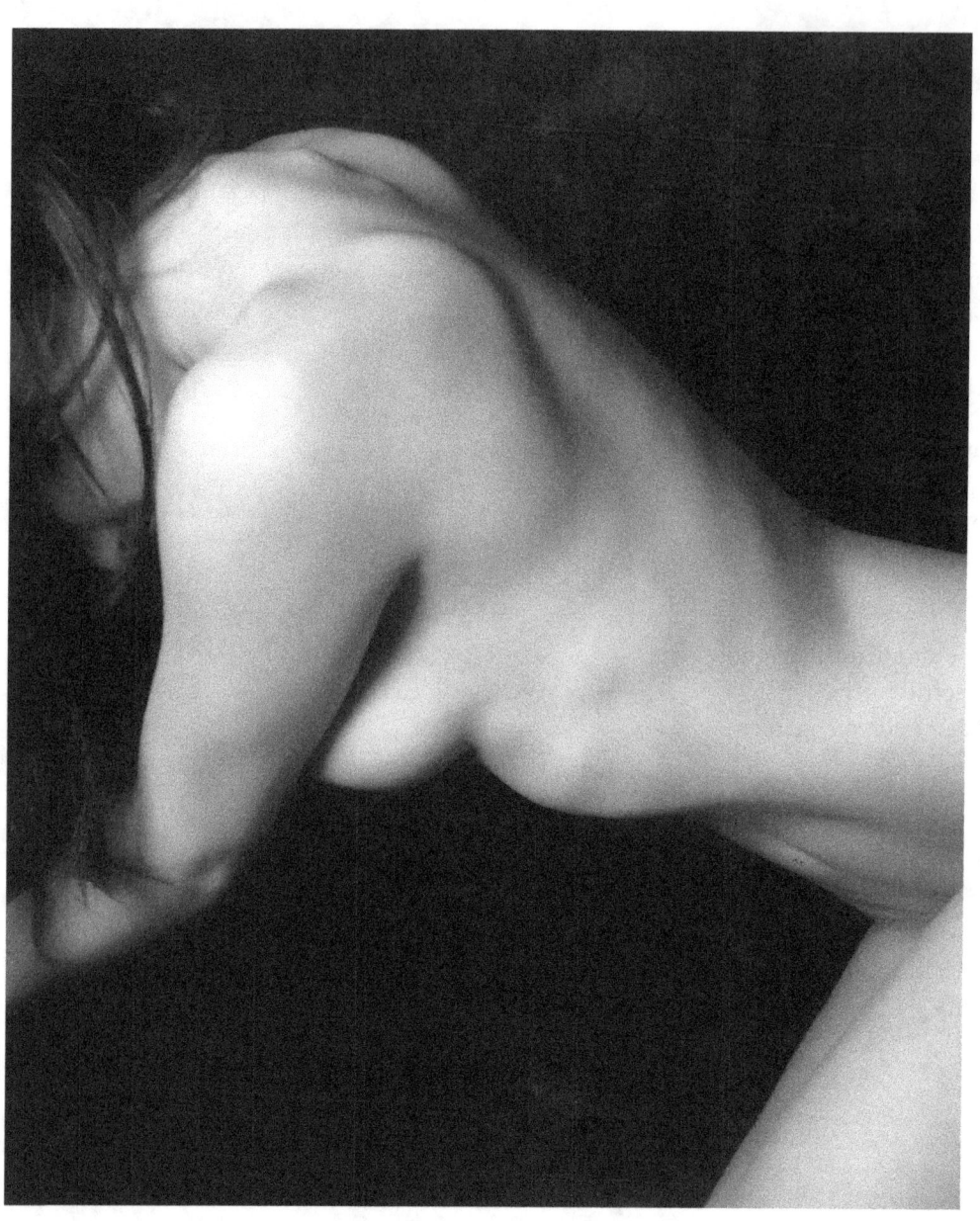

She bent
Effortlessly
Her hands of tiniest ivory
Fumbled with the lock
And summer's brazen air
Held the intensity of promise

A drink? She asked.
Yes, oh yes.
Preferably of you.
I thought as
My black boots
Sullied the pristine floor
Of her kitchen

Later
Naked upon the floor
Her lips were wet with
Deception and desire
I kissed them

She laughed, then said
My husband will be home soon
I watched the dust from
Her gathered blankets
Dance in the dying sunlight

There's still some wine left, I said
Her response, "take it with you"
Was shadowed by her footsteps
Heavy and sad
Upon the bleached oak

Soon, I found myself
Walking the long, narrow trail
To the highway
Clutching the sweet Amarone to my heart
While thinking that the night
Was failing to taint
The beauty of summer

And that life would struggle impotently
Yet fail to taint
the beauty
Of love

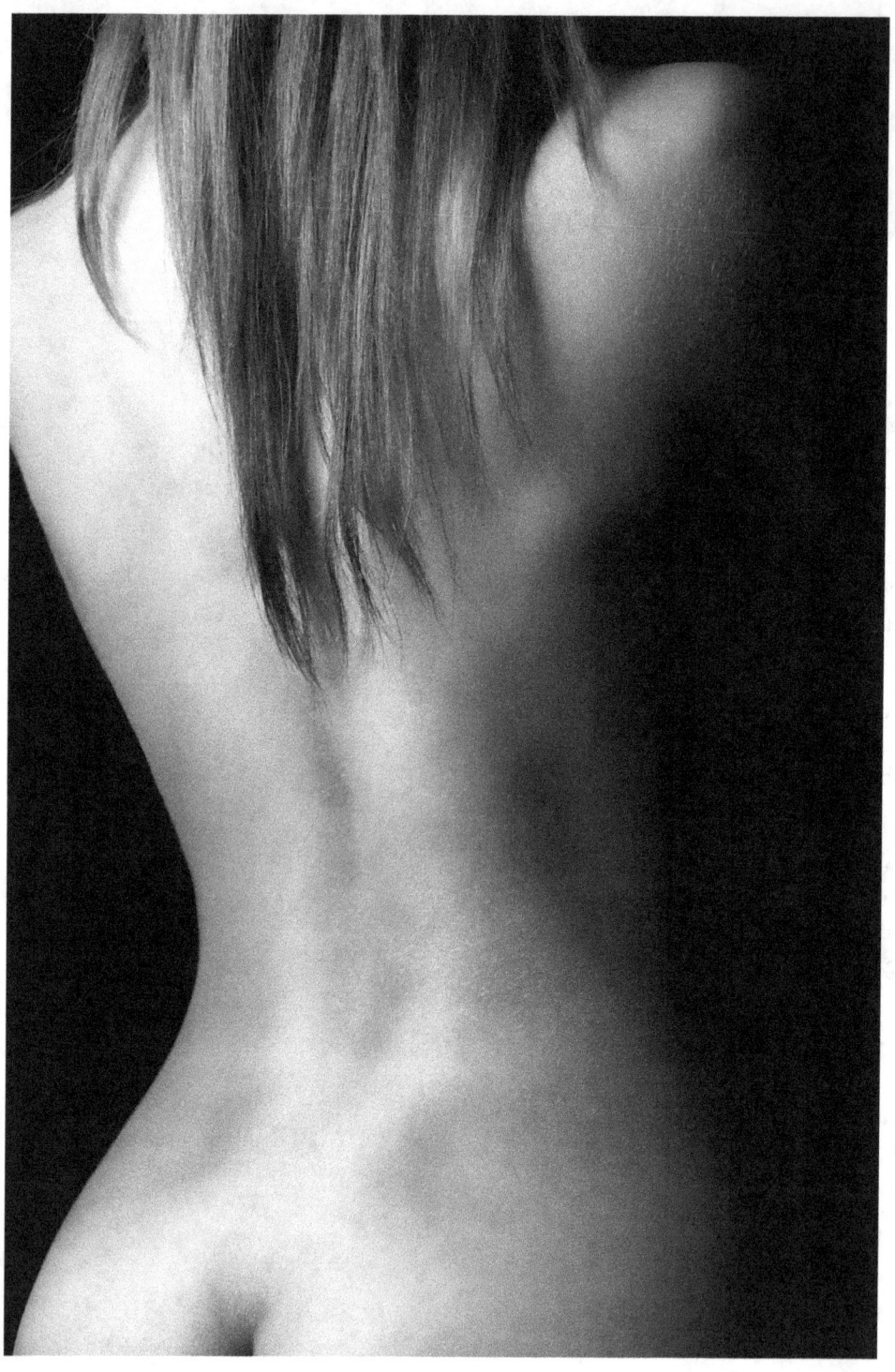

Your skin is a tapestry of artistic beauty, I said.

Is there any other kind of beauty? You said.

All artistry is beauty, waiting on you to drink of its lure.

To drink in it, you said.

I thought

Sometimes flowers come from within. They leave us speechless. Drowning in so much beauty that it

Bleeds through from our own lacerated roots
capturing us, like children
in the opening orchids that scented the night

Later, since we could not escape, we fell into sleep
the scent of the orchids
a part of us forever.

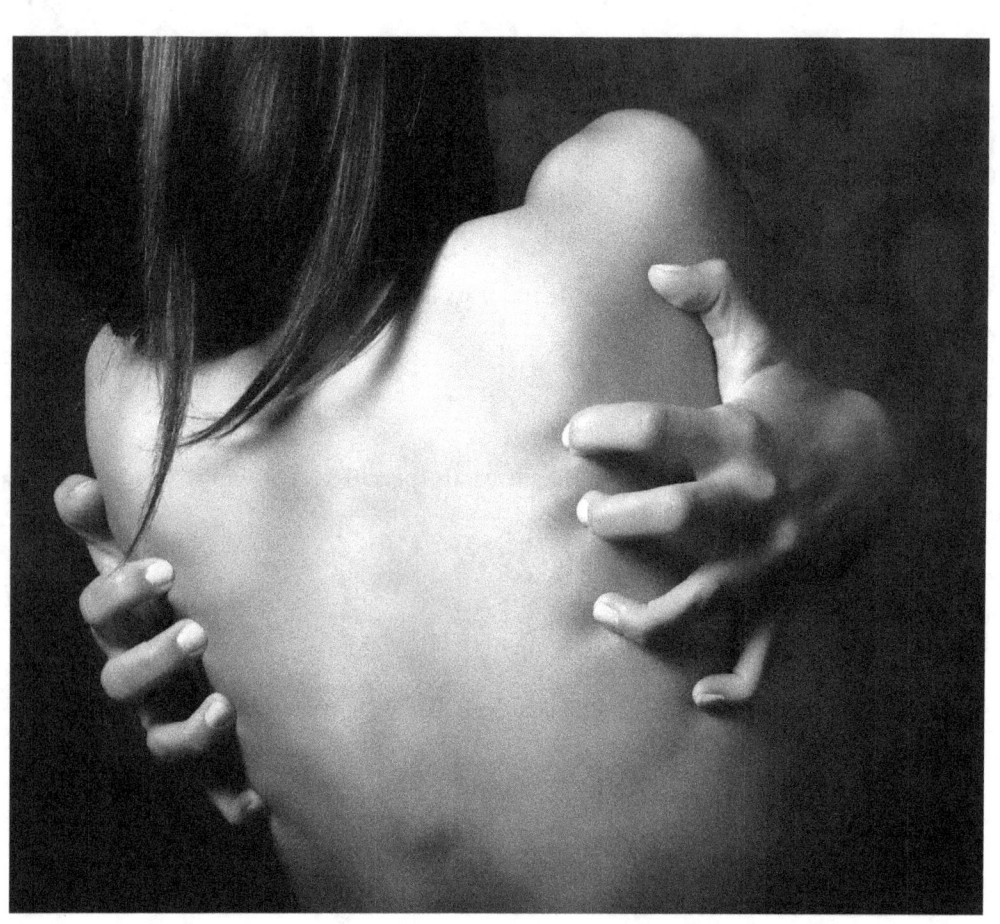

There are figures on the Allen Wall
Forgotten words and images.
Graffiti. Blood.
And three-foot white letters
"I still love you Jane".
I loved her too.

Cars weave in broken synapse
Beneath the barrier.
Unaware of our love for Jane

And we take comfort
In our ignorance
Of the muted strangeness
Found written
In love's grand irony

Love amid chaos
Beauty amid death

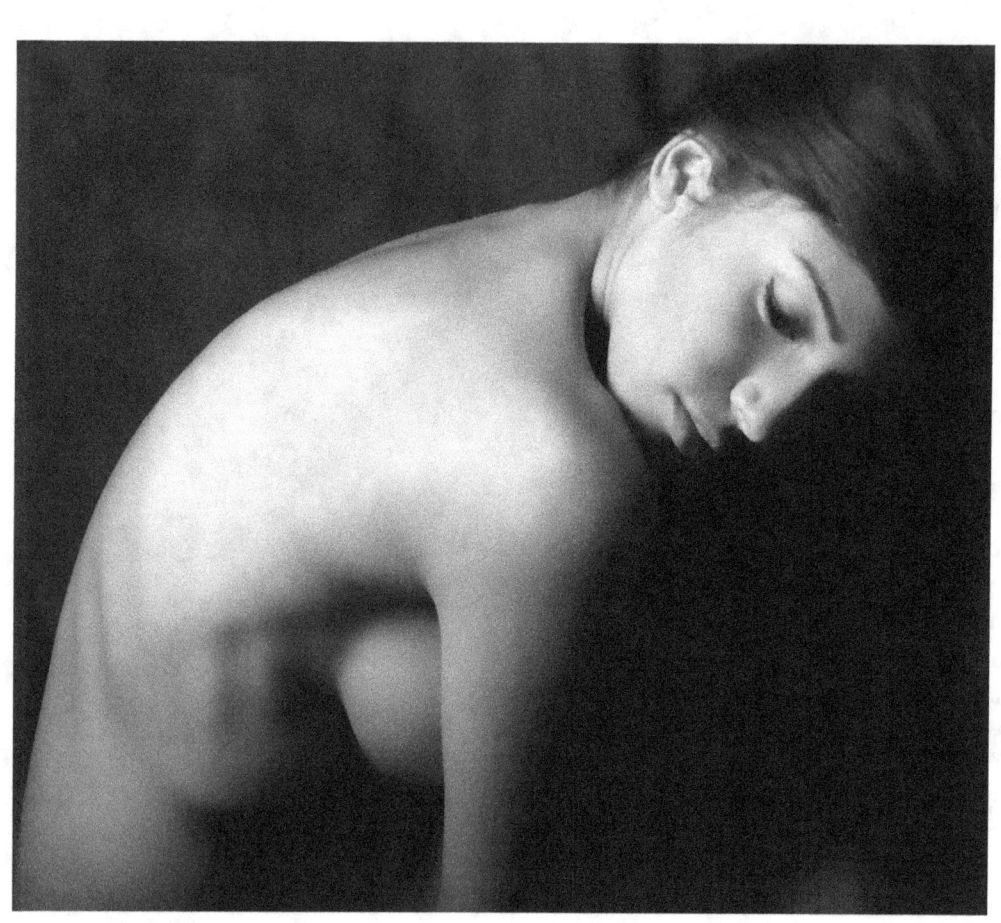

Among the wine bottles
She and I
Were laughing. Crazy. Drunk
The city, shuffled beyond the window
Impervious and maligned
To our blessedness.
Then she laughed again
And
In a sudden, quiet moment
I saw that her eyes were sad.

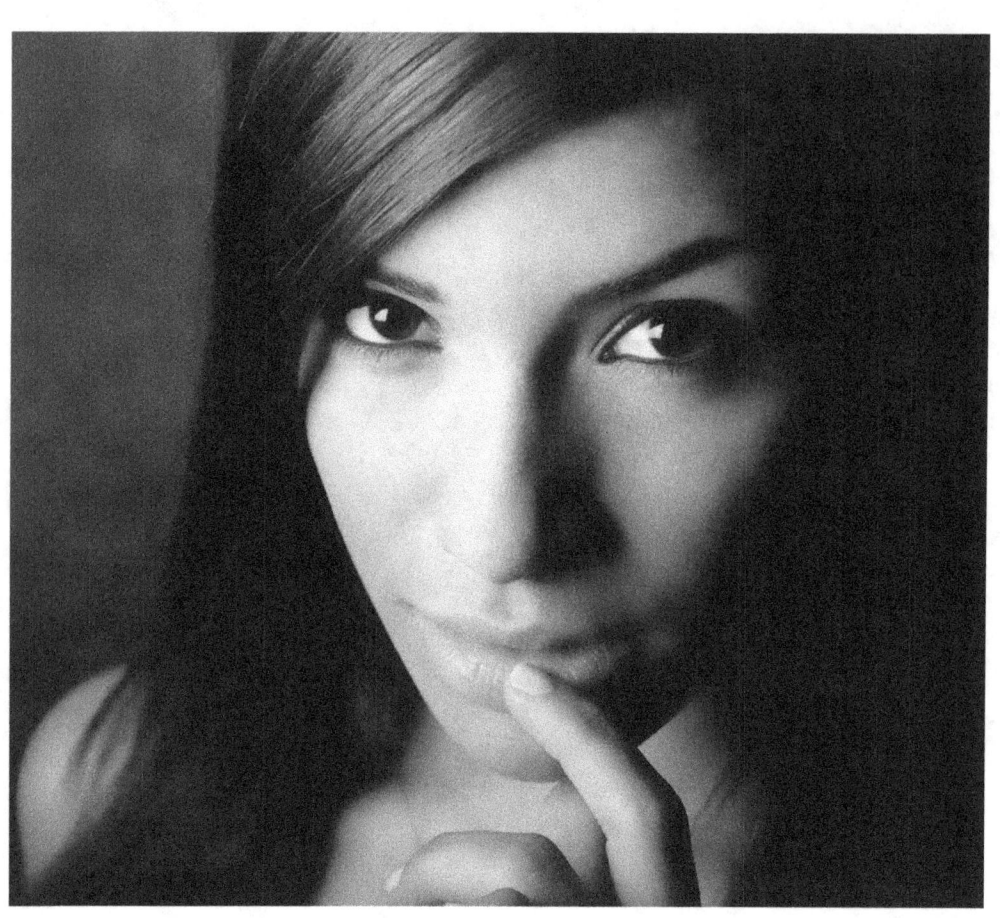

When your reflection danced
Upon the water
Of the copper fountain
In the Old Clock Hotel
I was taken for
But a moment

When we fell together
In desultory embrace
I was distracted and
Hardly noticed
At all

Later, in the cafe
I commented on the wine
But not your
Eyes

If I knew I would not see you
After that day
I would have said:

That your lips
Faded in winter
Had forsaken none of their
Beauty

And

That I envied the
Ripe and scarlet berry
Caressed gently by your
Tongue

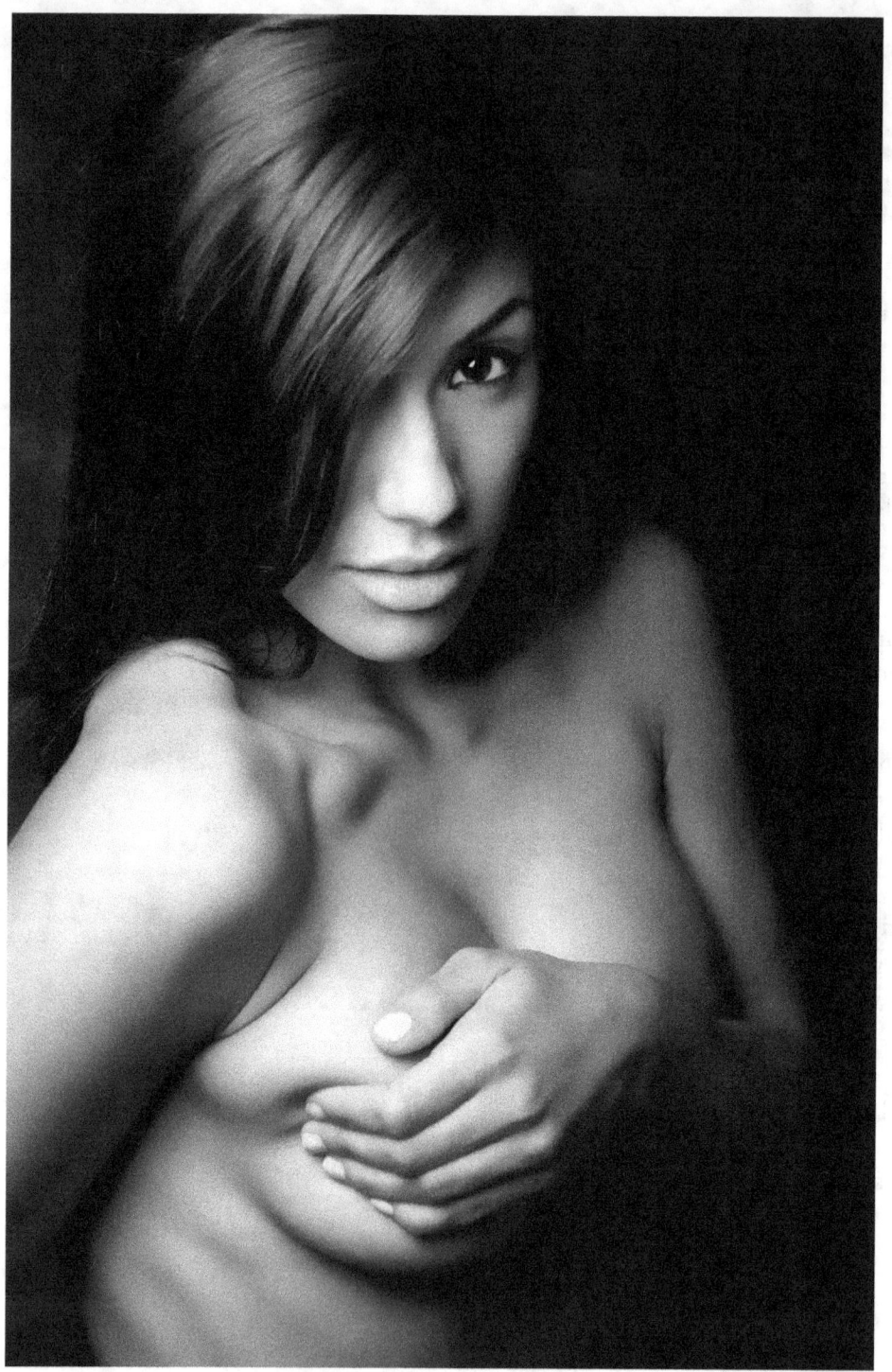

On this
Loneliest of days
In shadowed April
The artifice of shelter
Does not hold me.

The soft
Lull of traffic
Though deceptively serene
Make indistinct
Love's reminiscence

But does nothing
To diminish
Your forceful beauty
The rain falls
Defeated

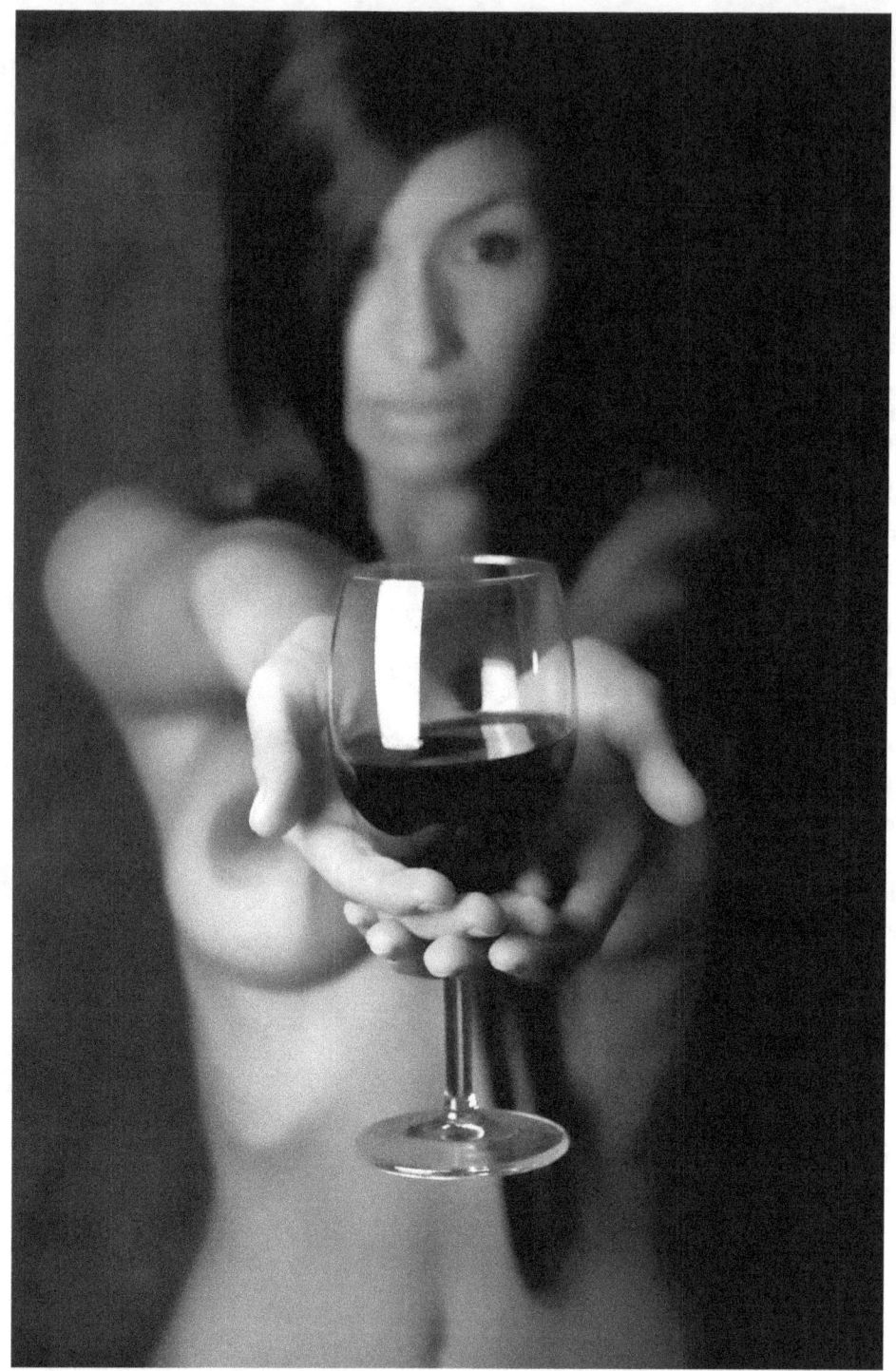

How much wine is too much?
She asked

Her Question
Poised and serious
Though I thought
Rhetorical

Naked
But for the bedsheets
She wore with
Quiet Dignity

Unfailingly
The heiress
Of my fumbling, strident
Desires

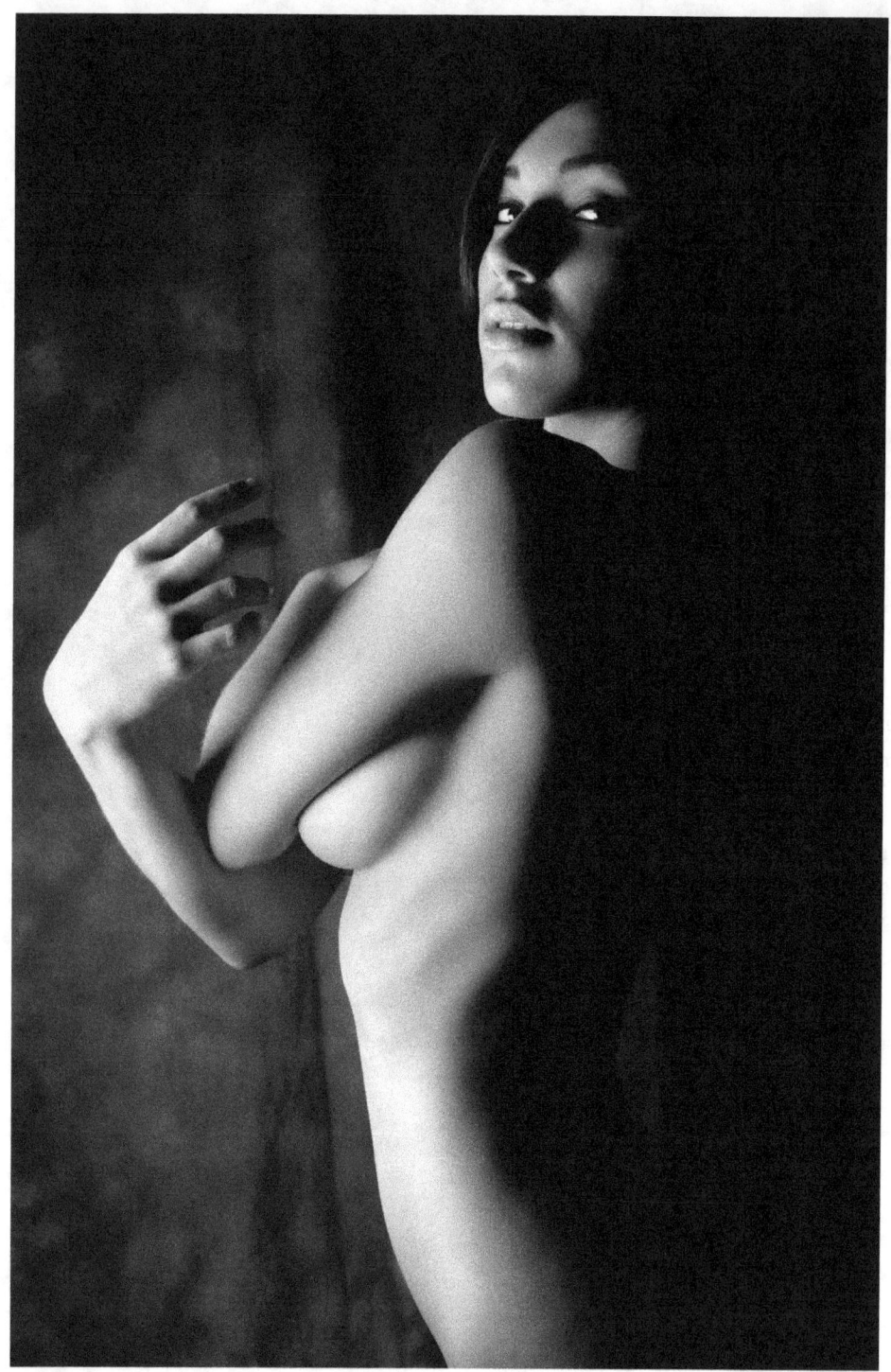

You seem to have
Spoken of me
As a judge, articulating his
Hollow mercies
Upon the condemned

I, who have worn your costumes,
Stood upon your stage
Reading of your broken lines
Stale with promise

I, who not long ago
Stood upon these very steps
And listened to the sad wail of traffic
Echo your mournfulness

You have desired
A creation in your image
Strange and human God
Your death rattle shriek
Is flooded with sad vanities

You will not hold
This poet, who defiled and,
Drunken, yet sublime
Discards the rusted flecks
Your philosophy affords

I, who was born,
In country pale and feeble
Am not anemic with
Its culturally thin blood

You are mistaken
If only in your belief
That I resonate
The empty, gluttonous howling
Of my supposed national legacies

I, for this reason,
Am grateful
That the spirit of my drunken flesh
Has rewarded me
In kind

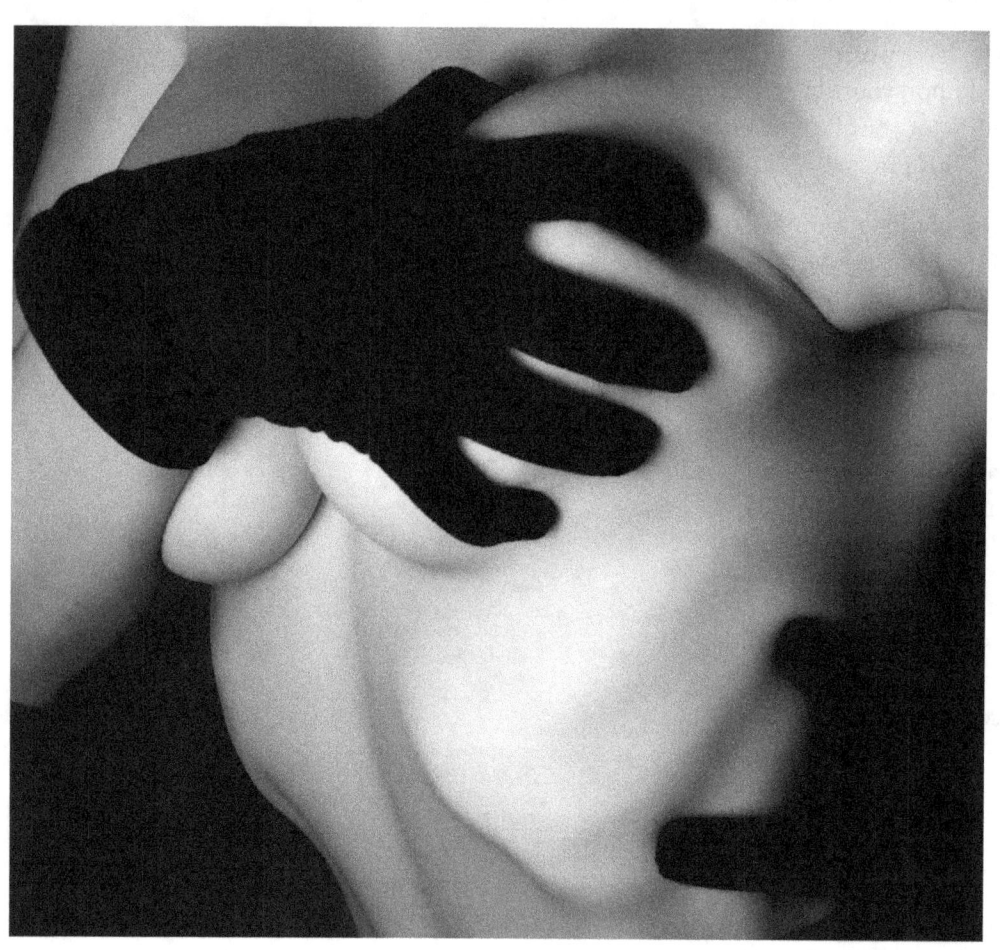

Let me look
Upon this trinity of beauty
A poet condemned
Before the fair selection
Of countenance

Each flower
Would tend to drown
Passionate ambition
Beneath the sensory exaltations
Of vision

The evening
Sad with desire
Bounds me ruthlessly
Within my unavoidable preference
For your
Incendiary
Heart

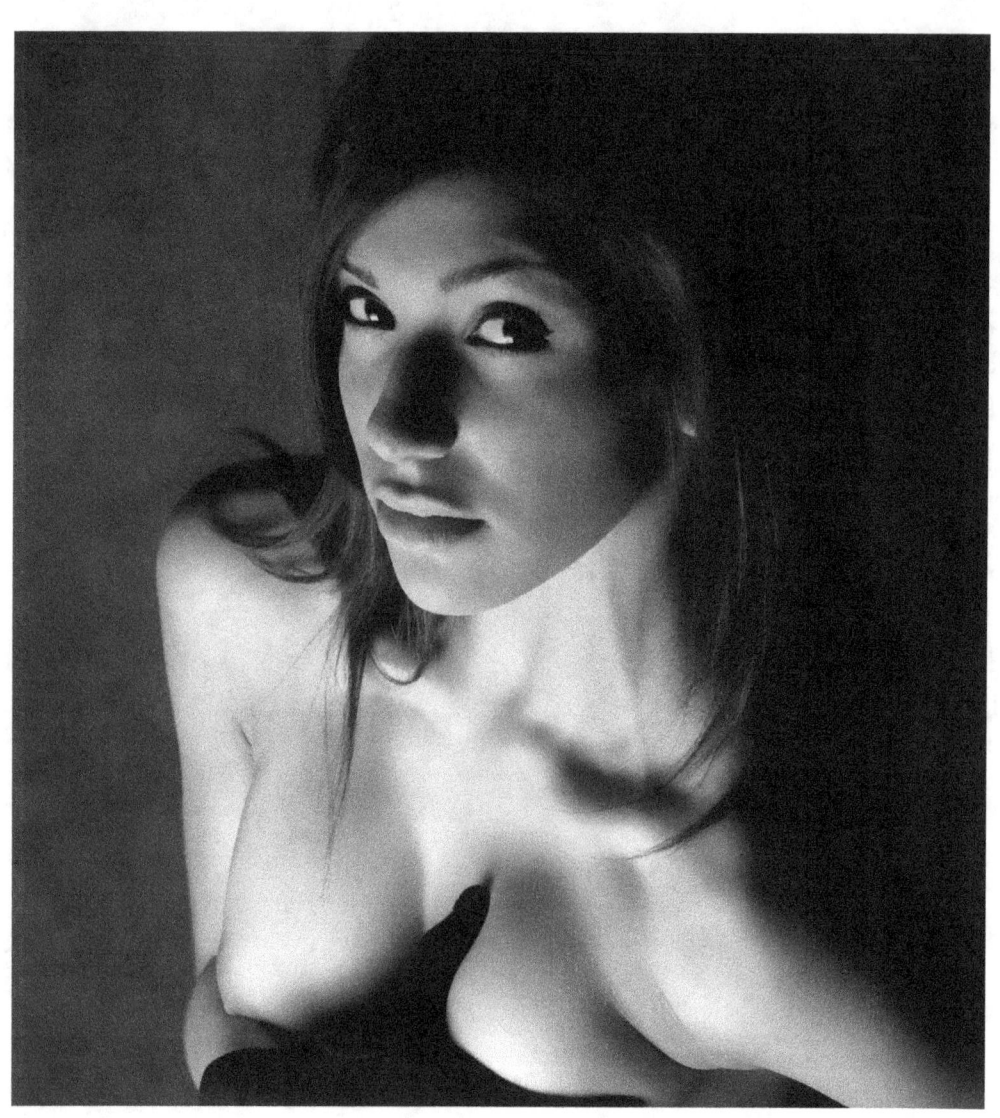

We all desire
The delicate tortures
Afforded by love

Seeking refuge
In poisoned flowers
We grasp and crave
Its sickened fevers

The kiss
Of its sweated whip
Upon our flesh
Consumes the sanity

Leaving us
A faded lyric
In the elegies of
Regret

And you, yourself
Ran your hallowed tongue
Along the contours
Of my chest

And drowsily
remarked upon
The sweetness of
My blood

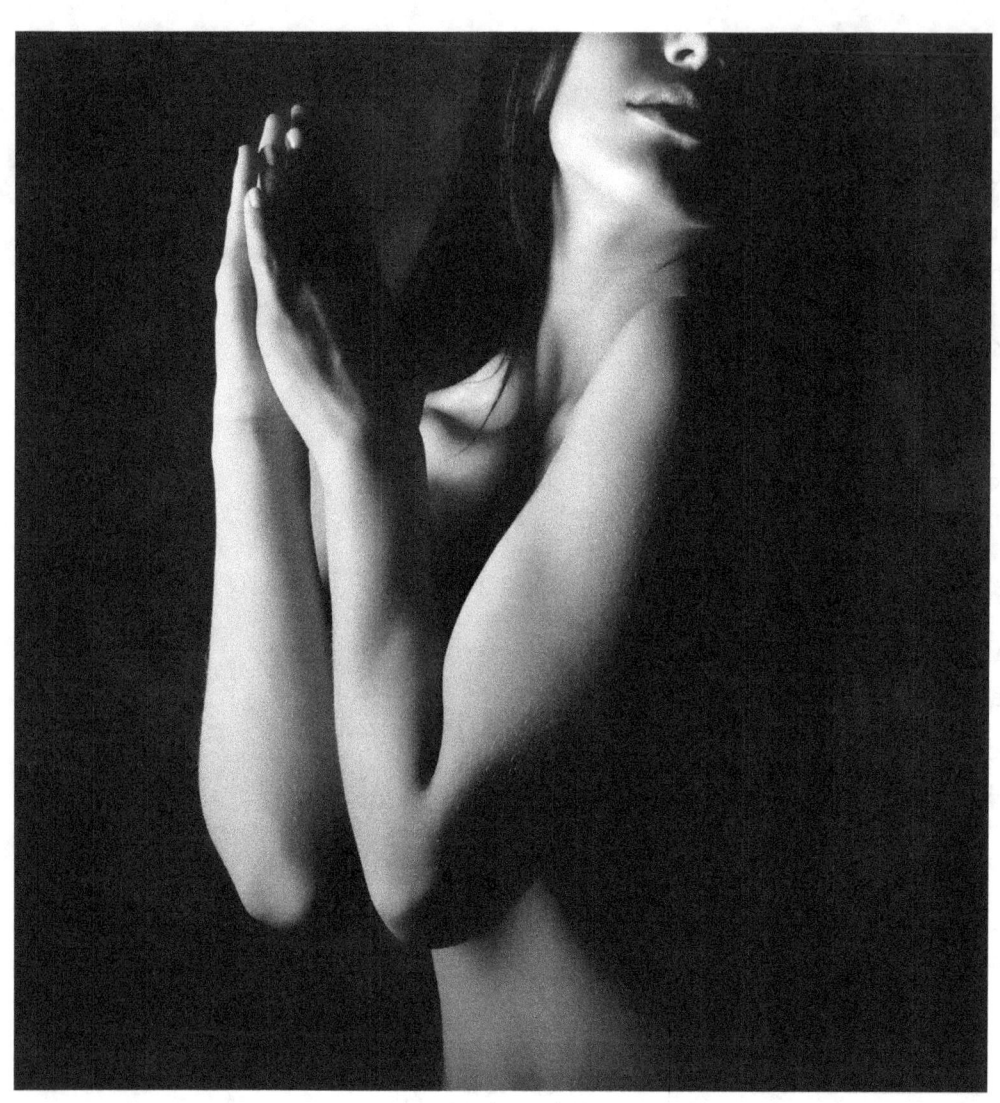

Summer's daughter
O sweet and naked
Mistress of nature
Wearing the glow of earth
Upon her beautied cheek
Her feet touching
The blankets of heaven
In sensual reflection

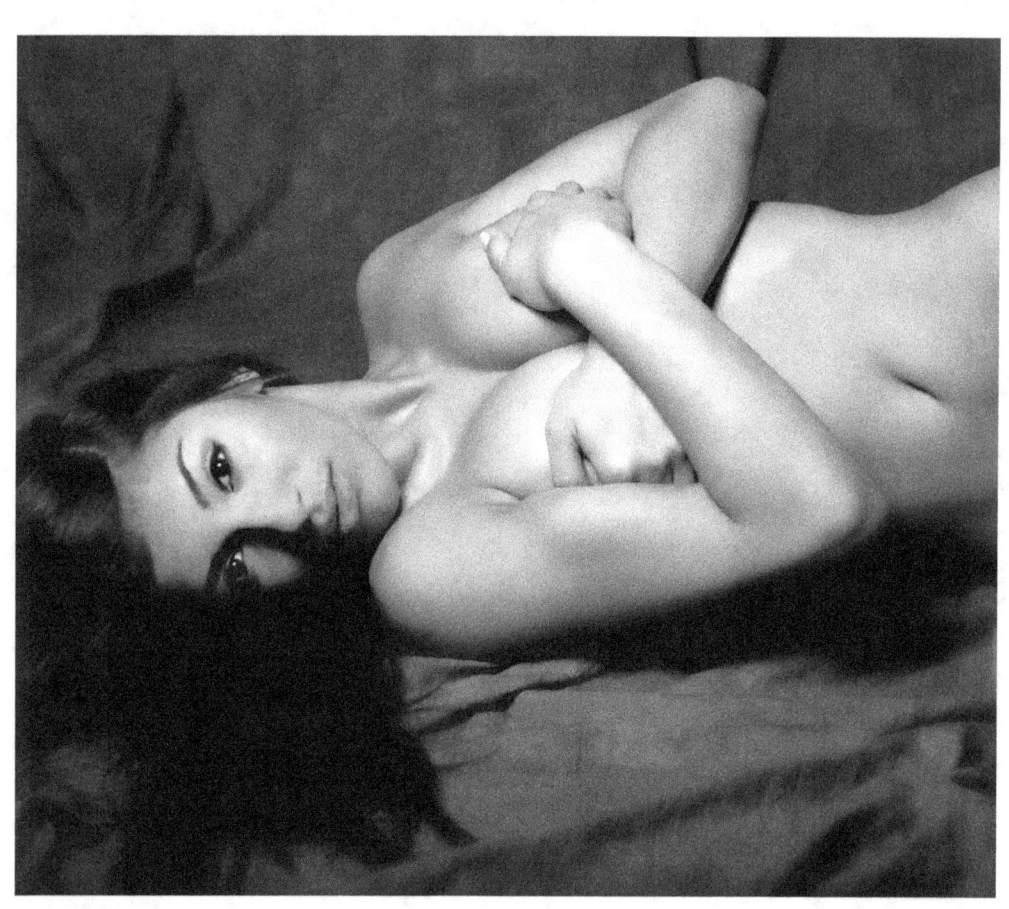

Friday comes
And scatters upon streets
That reek of
Savage melancholy
As my distortions
Are cast forth from
The drunken eyelids of
A wounded lover

Shadows shall claim refuge from
The winter's bleeding sun
In this drowsy hollow
Untouched by the intrusions of
Exaltation and light
My wine-stained fingers
Gnawing restlessly at
Hopeless corruptions

Insanity's feast
Is laid in brutal honor as
Death stoops to claim her
Hallowed Knighthood
Adorned in flesh
With laughter now
Shaking me woken
In holy confusion

My visions torrential
Though lighting the strange atmosphere
Her quietude presence
An open lotus
She delicately removes
Her tiny coat and
I am caressed in permanence
My heart in belief

That

Even the saddest of days
Can own moments of
Purest beauty

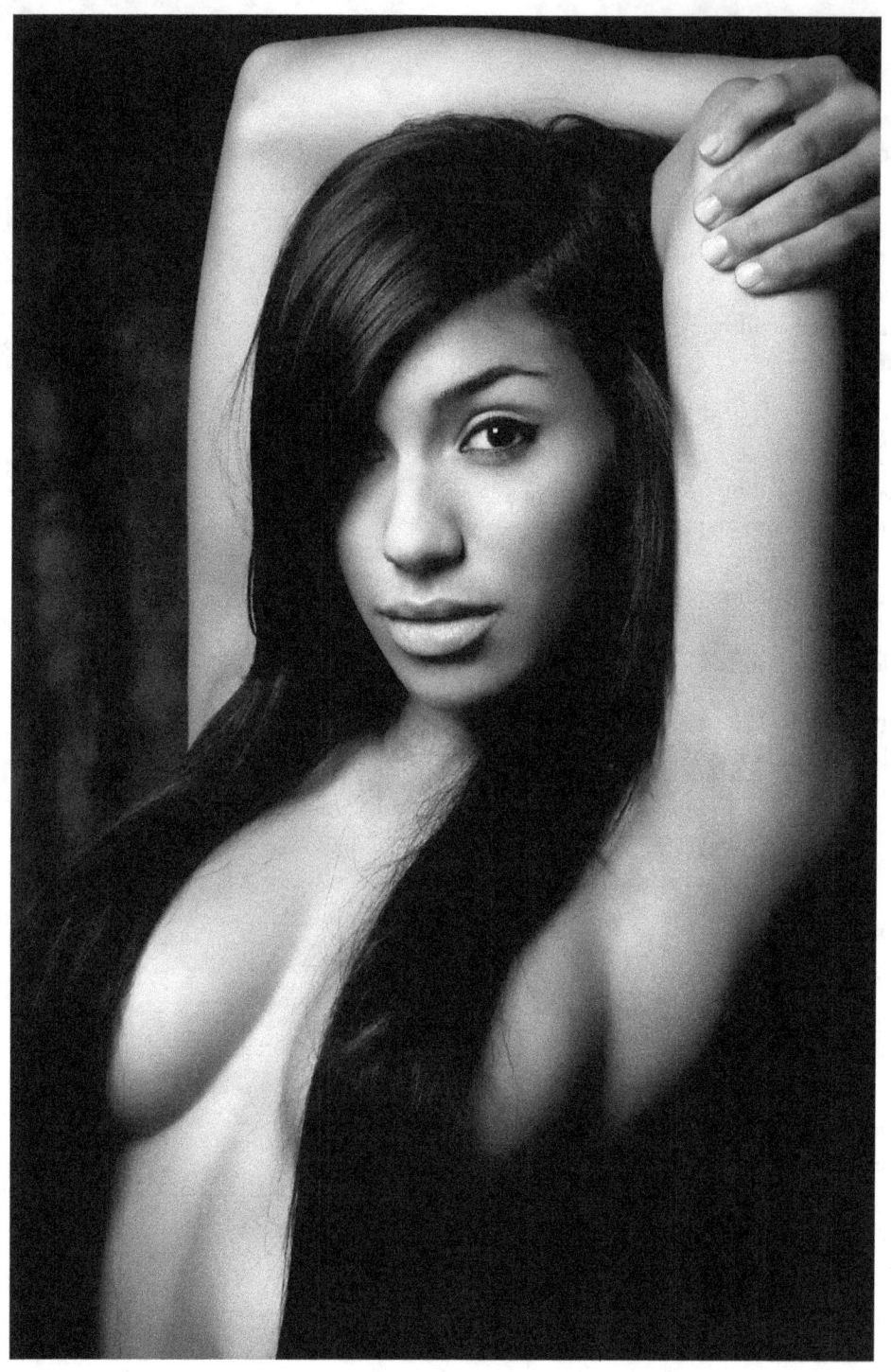

Paula, I remember
The delicate pallor of
Your childhood face
And soft smile laced with sadness
Belied your false innocence

I can see your hazy shadow
Behind the screen door
A petal among
The strange flowers that fell
In the evenings of summer

Though our woods, now
Lie as raped and tattered
As the boulevards of youth
The wounded tranquility in your eyes
Haunts me still

Time, you whore
I feel your insatiable hands
Rifle my clothing
As I lay drunken and passive
Upon the winter earth
A victim of your subtle thefts

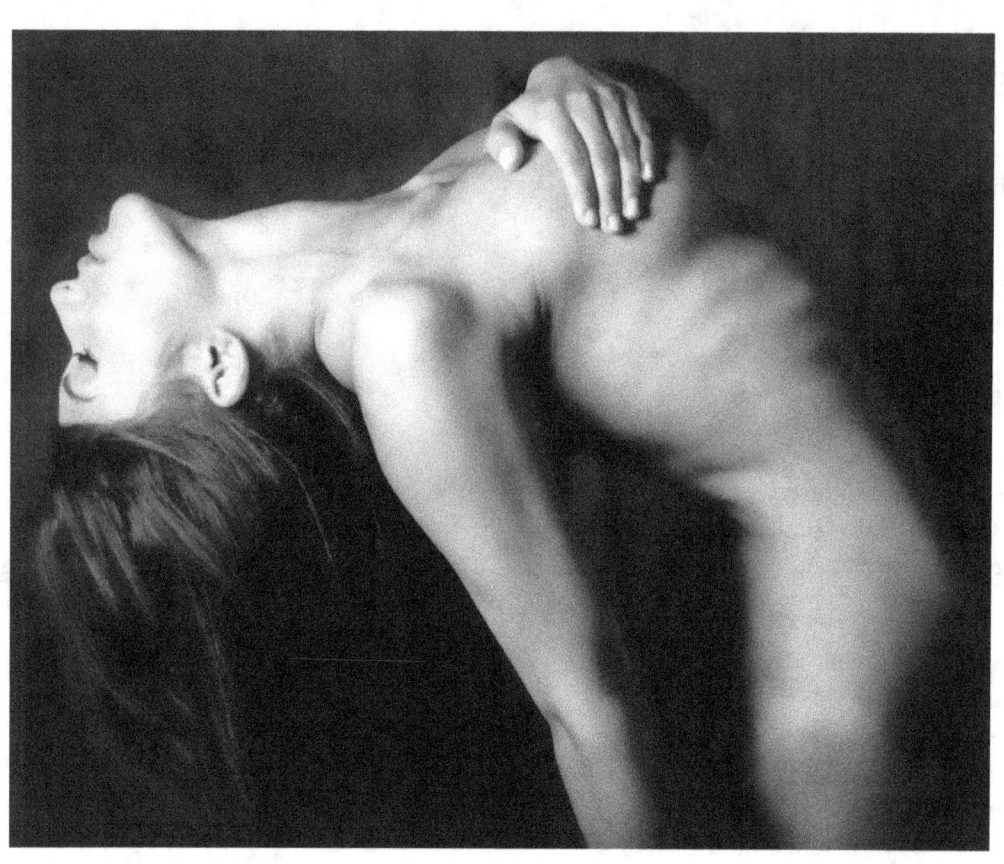

You appeared at my door
Masked in hyperbole
The ringing of telephones
Stopped and
Secret moments
Began

I loved you in September
The sun came purposely
Through the window
To lay itself upon
Your vigorous body
In silent conversation

To which you responded in kind
And I struggled with your beauty
My fingers, spellbound pilgrims
In the fragrant orchards of your longing
I overheard my muted voice say

I will uncurl your passions
Like trembling leaves
I will be mentor
To your hidden desires

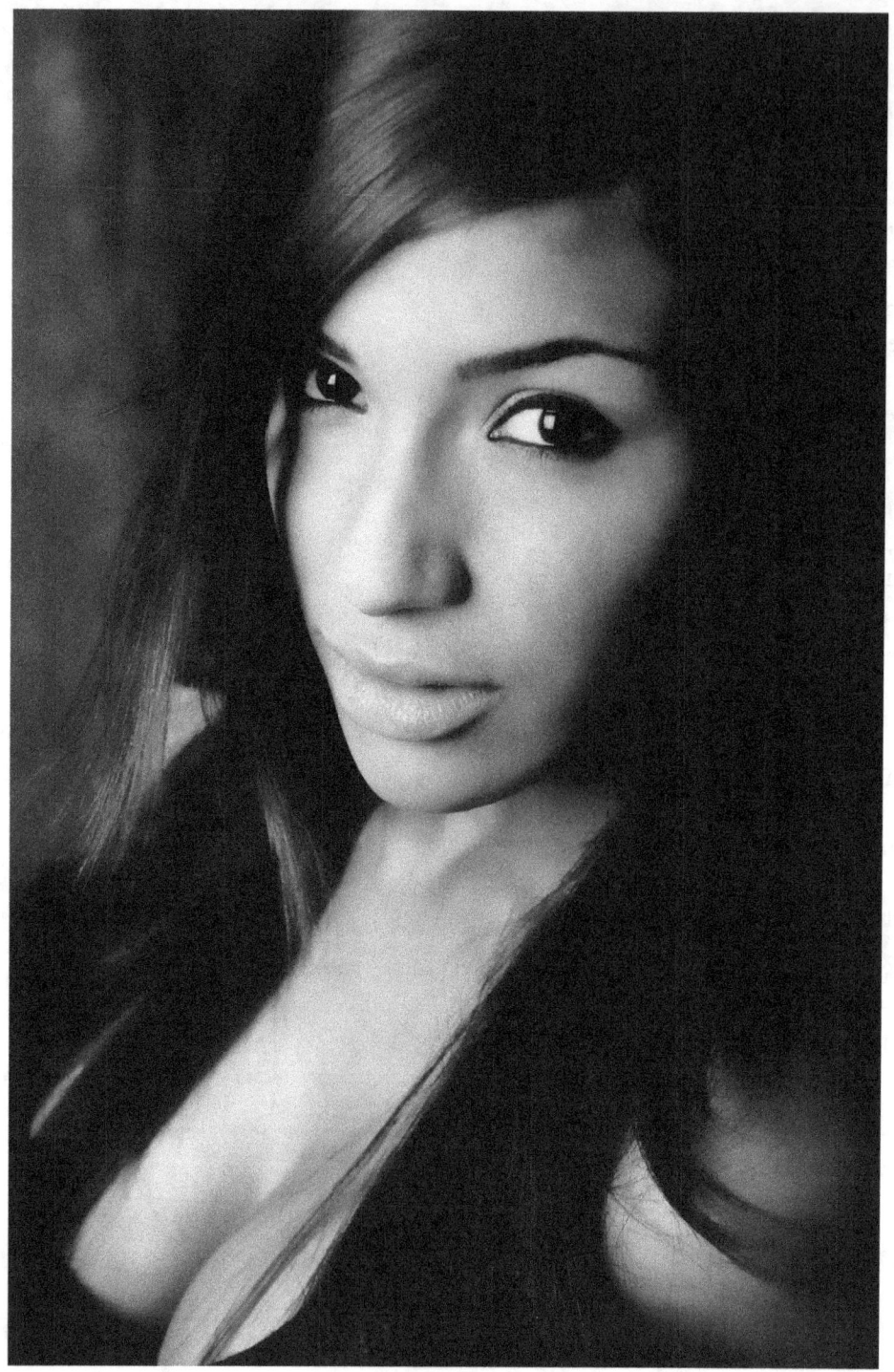

As she lit a cigarette
I saw her face in the
Crimson fireglow

Standing above the
Subway grates, and framed
In billows of steam

I thought that
She was the most beautiful thing
In that city

At 3 A.M.

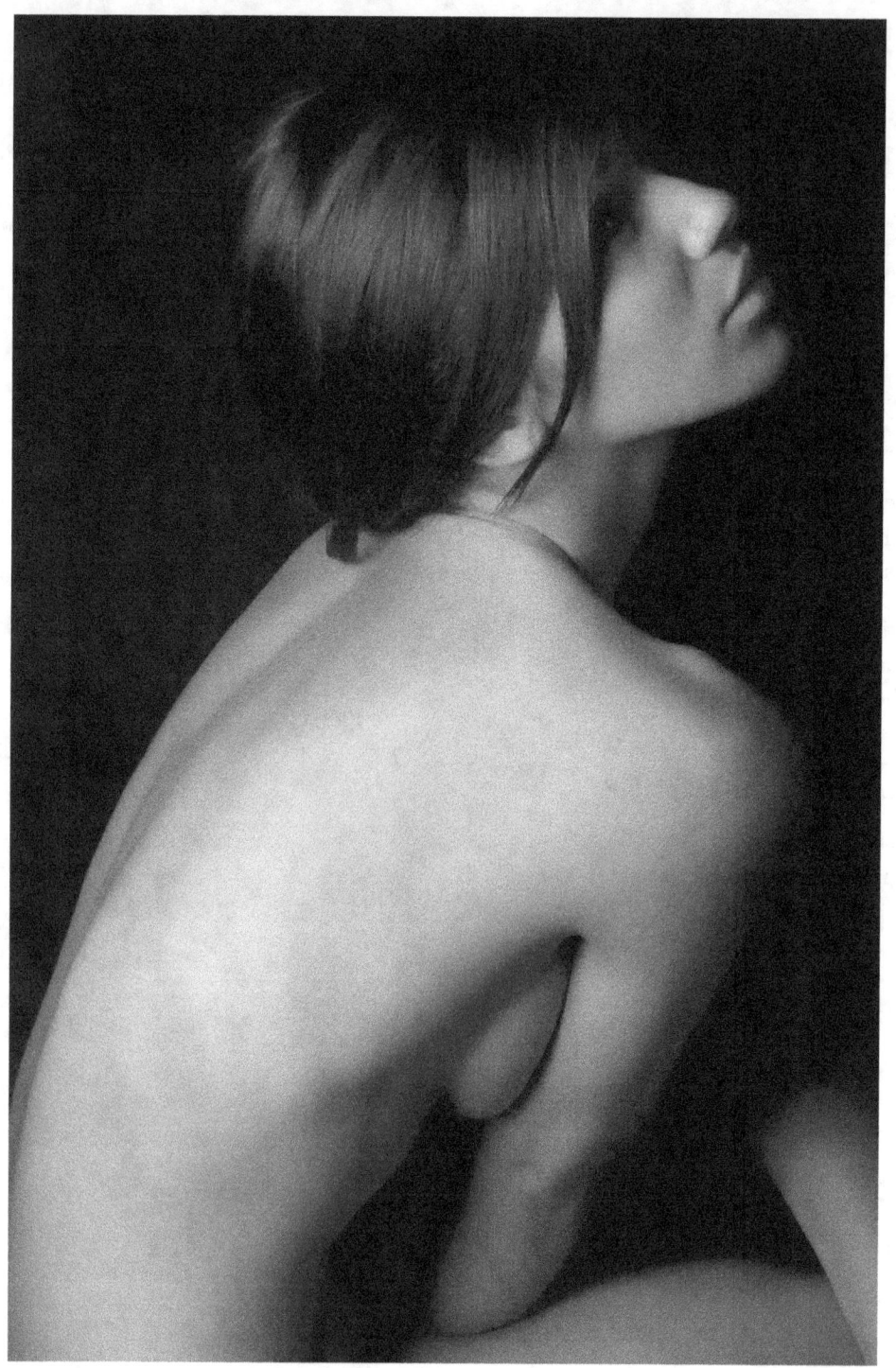

She said
"I'll be 36
In ten short days"

Marilyn
Bless her gentle beauty
Only made it that far

"Thirty Six"
She repeated
Like a funereal dirge
"What happened to the time?"

"Yes" I said
"The sweet voices
That carried upon
The surface of the lake
Are fading to a
Soft twilight whisper"

"And death,
Waits peacefully
Beyond the
Blood Horizon"

"That's so depressing"
She said
Attentive now

"No" I said
"Death is kind
And persistent
In its reminder
To adore the moments

Soon to be reclaimed."

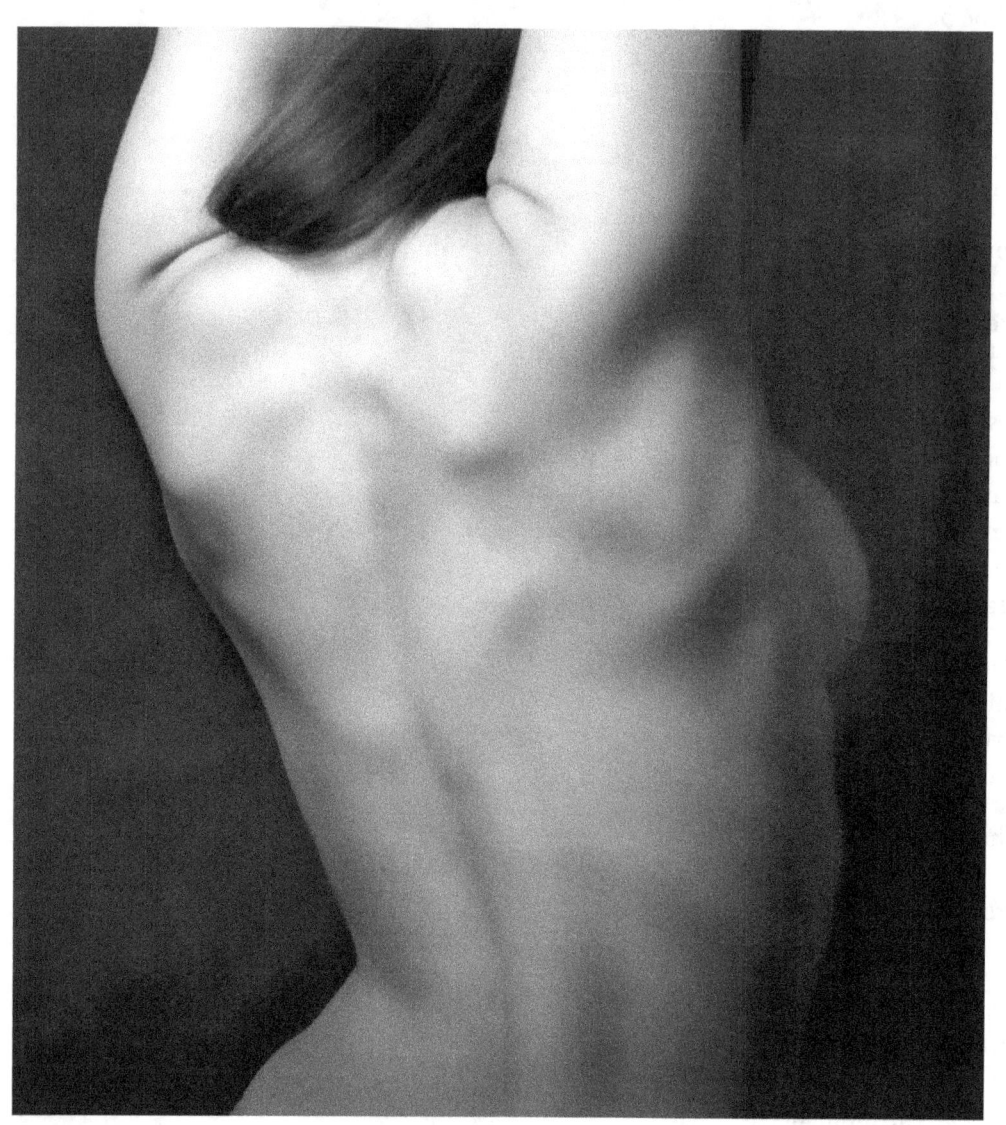

I can see the faint light in the window
Of the house that cast its shadows long and bleak
Upon my conscience, bludgeoning me
To walk slumped upon the brick laid sidewalks
While in the peripheries of sight
Ghosts would linger in velvet cradles
Waiting to occupy the decaying bones of youth

Within the minds of the condemned
It is said that freedom reigns supreme
And I, too can swear upon these truths
They run silently as rivers in the blood
To rise and overflow along the banks
With the languid moon hushed
In the suffering midnight sky

I would seize my chest in terror
Amidst the paralysis of nightmare
As in vision I lunged weakly
Toward the bleeding torrents
My flesh was torn upon the salted earth
With echoes of Miserere dying
In the desiccated chambers of voice

Now the light is ashen
The broken dawn spills between
Houses, resting in decay
And along the emptying streets
Specters prowl the soiled city arches
Though burdened with fear they fall gently
In hushed retreat

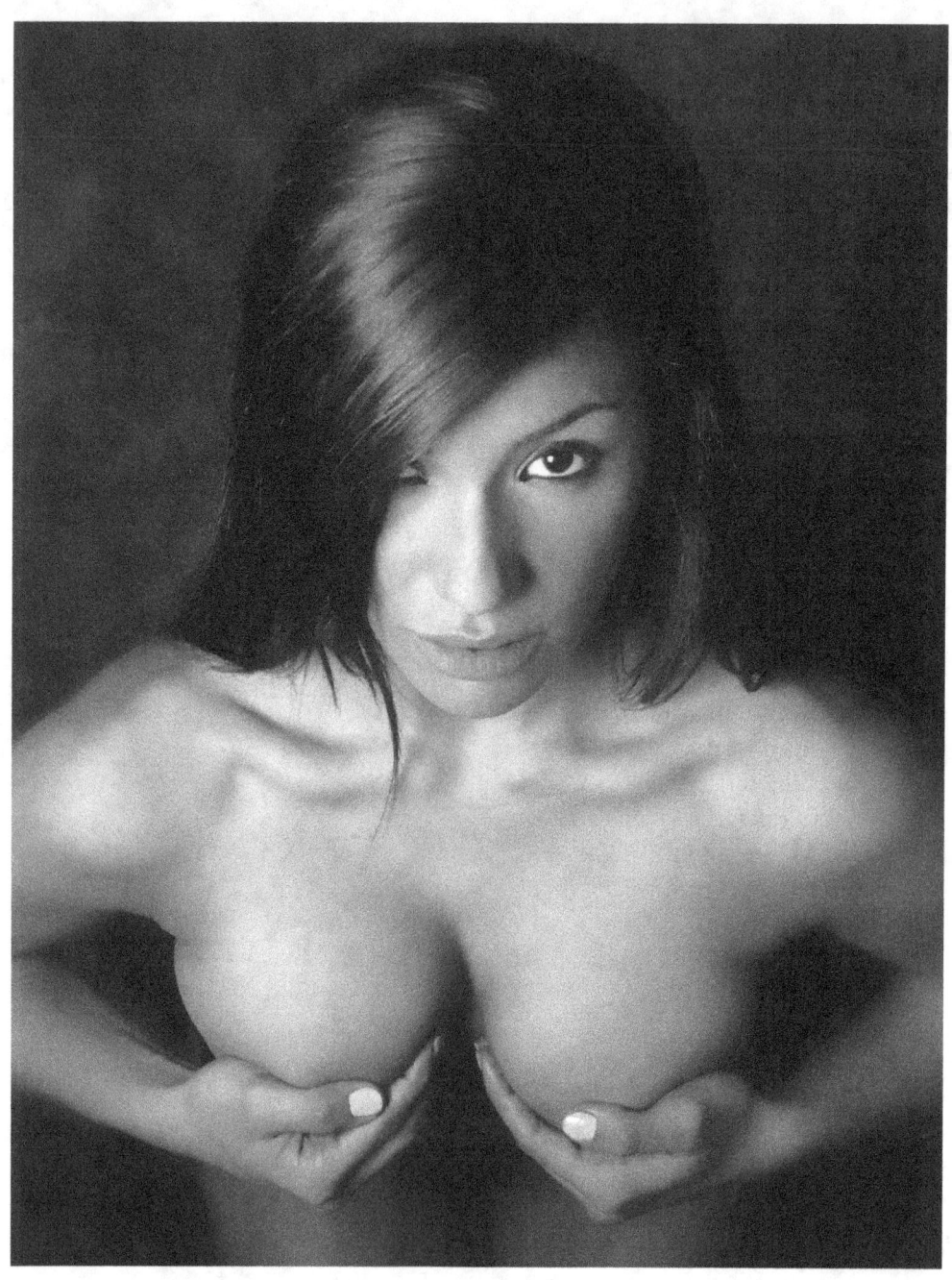

The wail of night, in death
Stretched into soft-grey sky

And she told me to leave

Her bedsheets scattered
Like bleached bones
With the bottles
Upon the floor

Remind me
Why I am here,
At all
I whispered
But she was

Unamused

As
The great absurdity
Of Mornings
Was illuminated
With the lady
Prone to
Incessant thoughts

While the poet
Momentarily
Loses his power
And shuffles onto
The burning
Streets

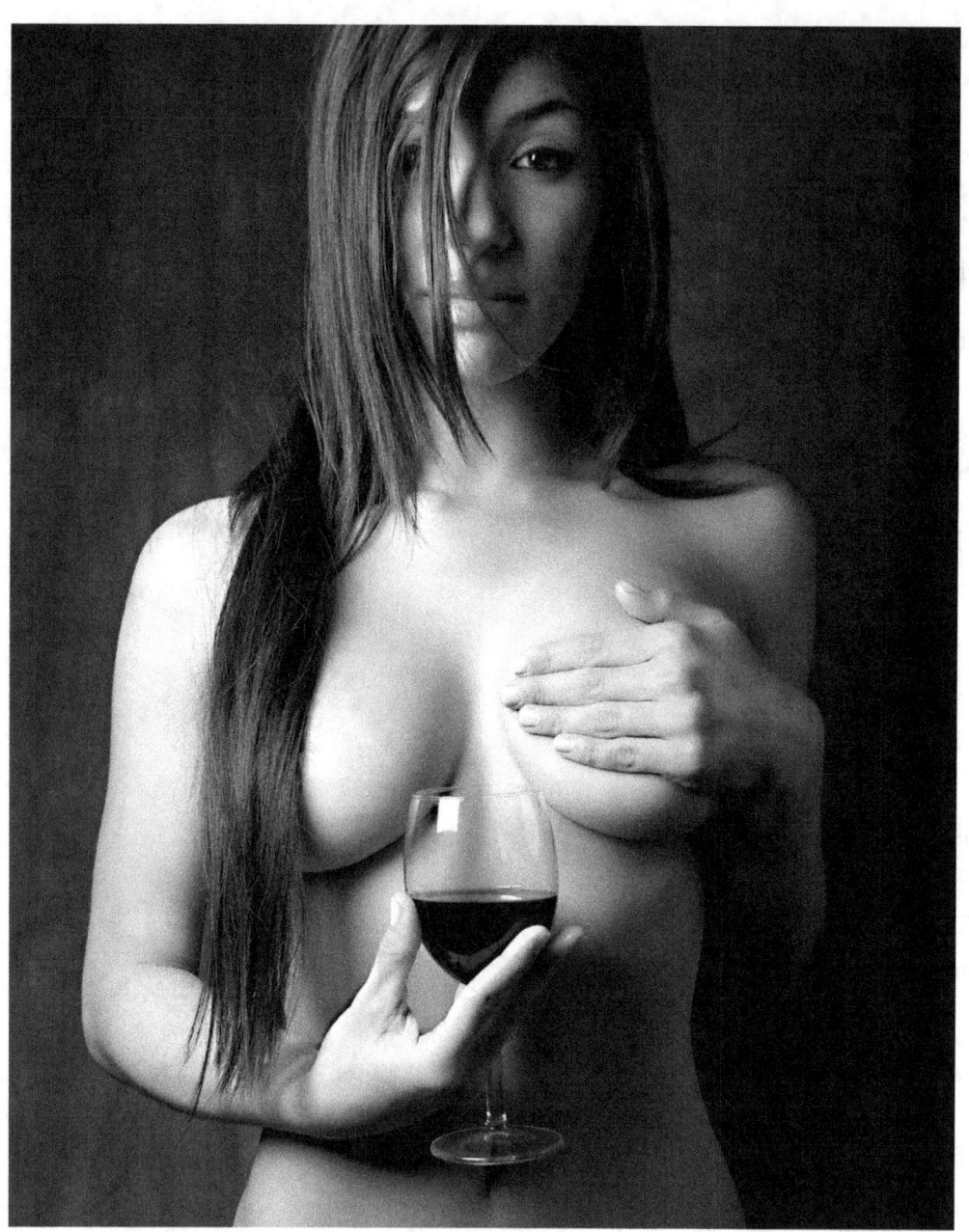

Upon my death
File silently down the fractured streets
And return, your arms weighted with wine
Let the bottles burn their amber shadows
Like tattoos, beneath your skin
In place of the hollow recollections
Forced upon you

Upon my death
Concede defeat to passions
Held upon your wearied breast
Let them carry you, unbridled
Into the arms of an open lover
Into a flesh untainted and wild
Absolved of illusions

Upon my death
Taste the lips of prose
For she will eventually appear
On the street corners of your existence
To steady you, as you rise to commence
Your stagger into oblivion
To join me

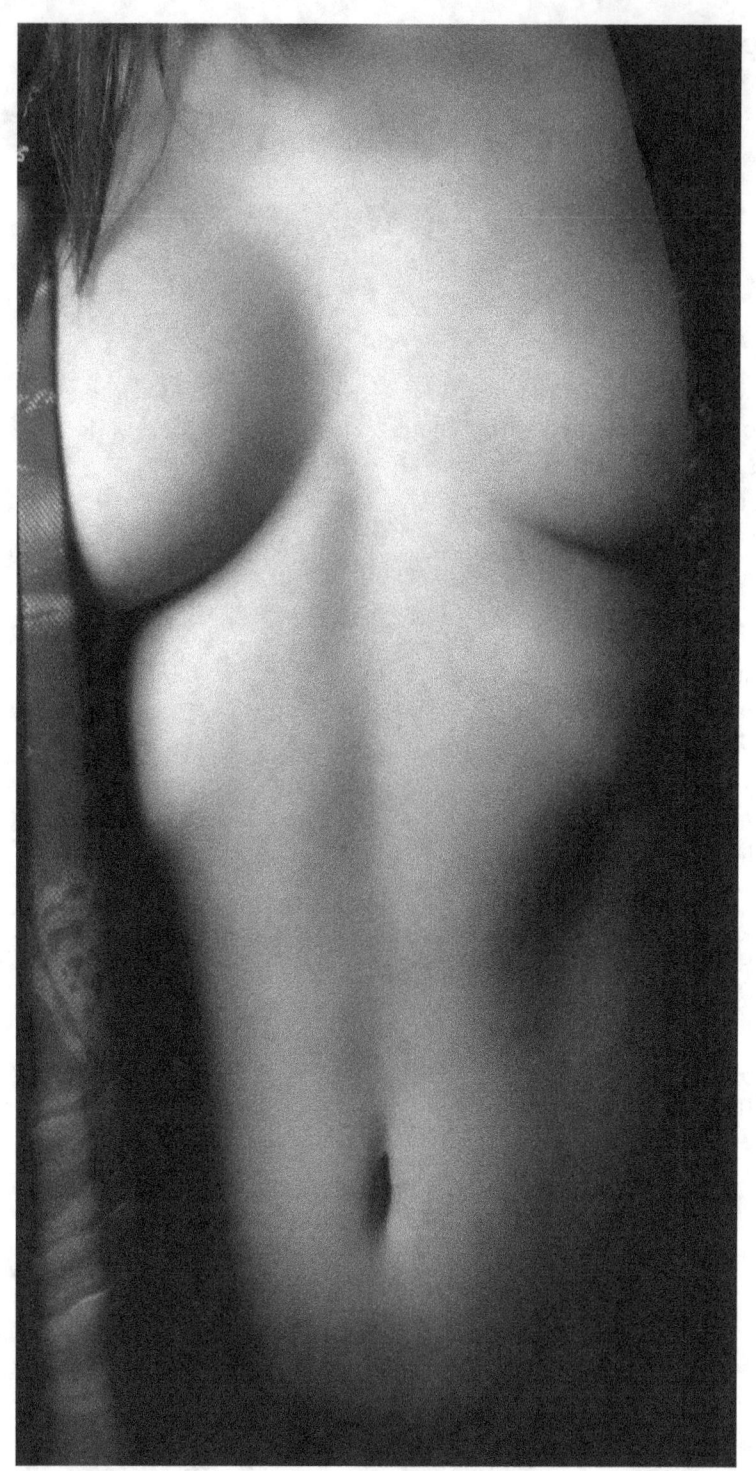

I do not drink of your poisoned offering
Your holy water is stained with duplicity

I do not mouth the empty rituals
That your sages bear upon their virgin tongues

I do not scour the pages of your canon
Forever to be stained with virtue's blood

You have tasted the communion bread upon your lips
And felt the empty sacrament burned upon your breast
Though your G-d shall not devour your flesh

I have stood inside your grand cathedrals
My feet upon the dusty stones
And eyes upon your revelation walls
Adorned in artist's tapestries of scorn
Held furtive from your covenant
Where kings lie tranquil in their blessed rot

I have seen your gilded beasts
Annihilate the blind philosophers of truth

I have dreamed the poet exiled from your cities
Consecrated in his grand illuminations

I have heard you torture broken whores
Thereafter taken to your beds in silence

I sway majestic in my untamed exodus
The mortal angel rises from the earth
I throw myself in rapture at her feet
And embrace the crumbling remnants of my divinity
By worshipping at the sacred altar of her thighs

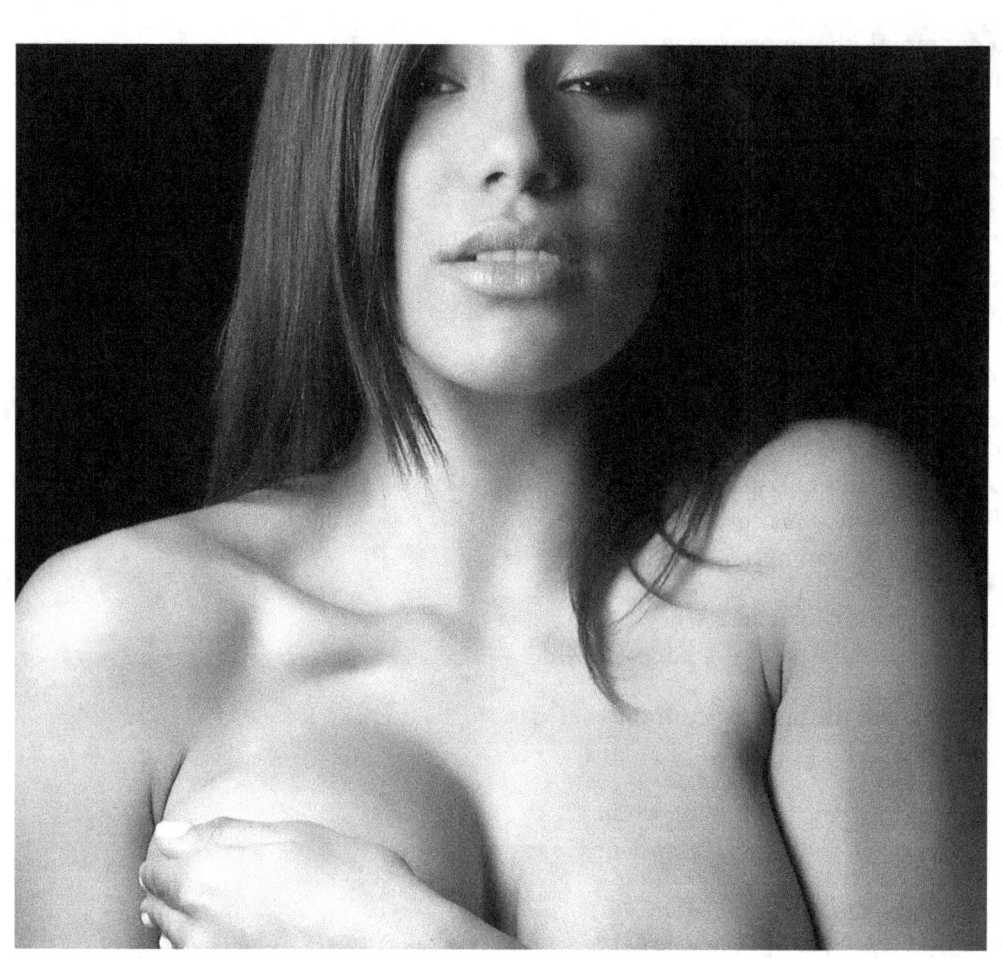

On your birthday
Tell your rhapsodic admirers
To abstain, this day of days
From drinking of your winter eyes.

That is to say nothing
Of lips, holding vigil
To finally conclude the trinity
With breasts, perfect and desired

Let their awareness fade
Unto the ever noble visions
Of a woman who ages
With passions unfurled

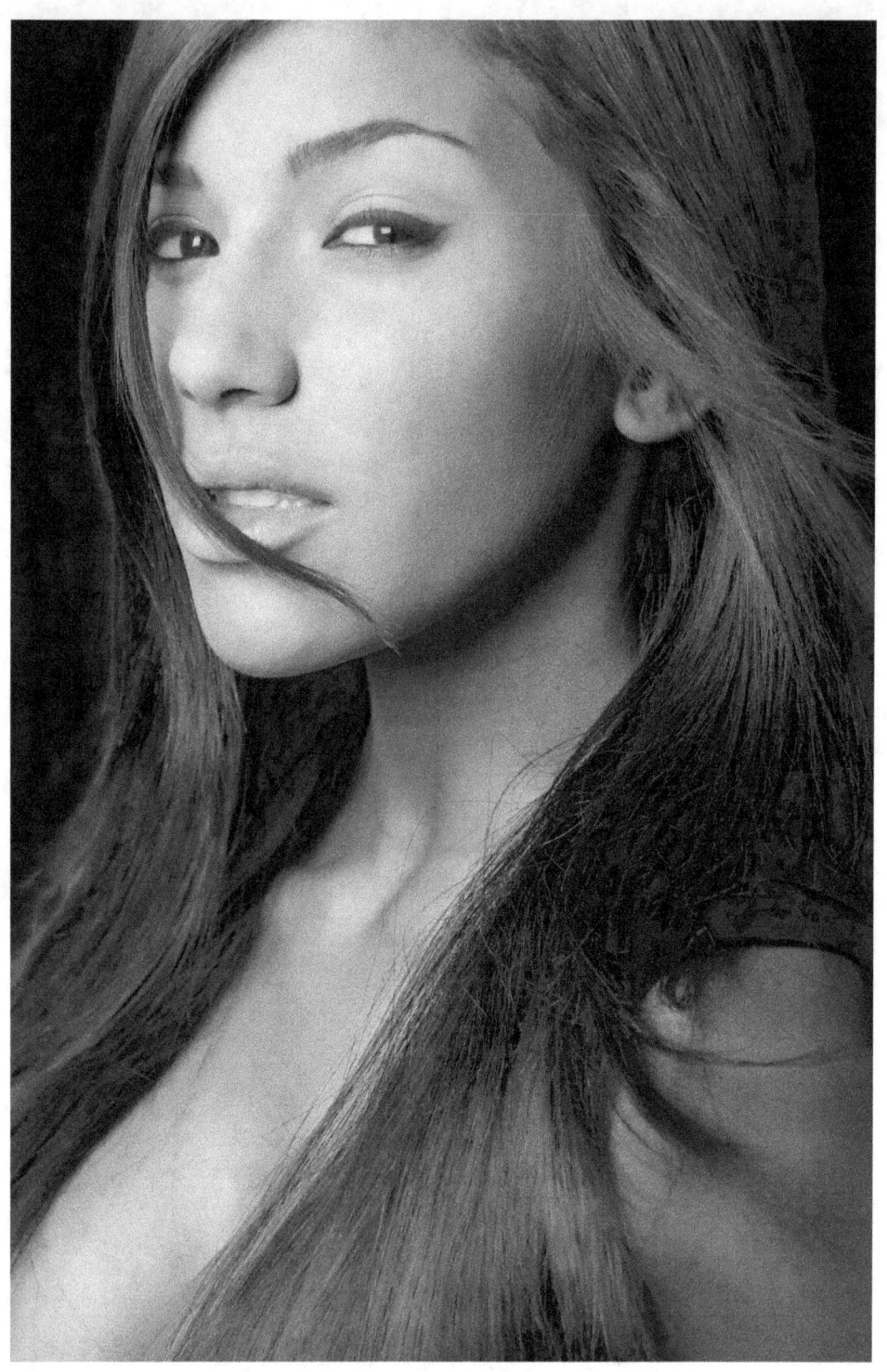

I remember Beth
Leaves in her hair
A gift from the trees of winter
When we walked in the park
The taste of snow upon her lips
Was gift enough for me

I remember Beth
She read Irving and leaned
Close to me
As I lit her cigarette
and inhaled the scent
of sweat and beauty

I remember Beth
When I walk alone
Touching my steps lightly
Upon the earth
So as not to disturb
The virtue of her memory

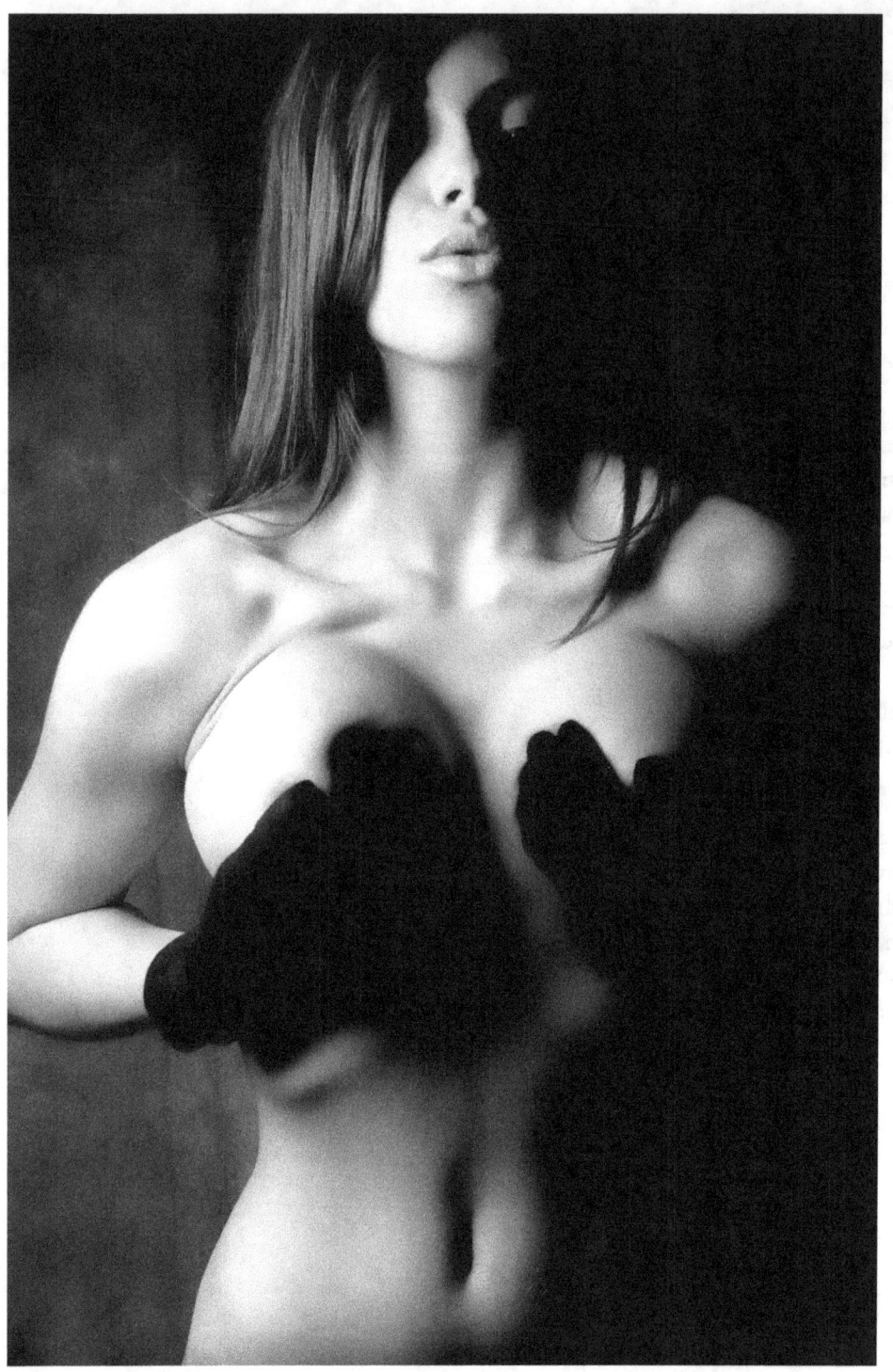

Your legs moved sweetly upon
The scorched sidewalk, then earth
The brutality of summer was at odds
With I, its putrid angel

I watched the city workers run
Their complimentary deceptions
From the grimy steps of
The Hotel Normandie

In the quietude of city afternoons
Time can flicker like candlelight
And realities of moments, lost forever
Are as heavy as the sweet, punishing air

So much of each life will
Crumble to beautified dust and
The most skilled archaeologist
Will never unearth your existence

But countless minutes had vanished
Since my eyes had found
Your legs, and followed you into oblivion
Or, the bar you entered at 9th & Main

Emptiness does not consider me a stranger
I am devoted to the warmth of darkness
You were amongst the scattered patrons
Where the neon sign flashed "open"

Again there were your legs and
A cigarette butt upon the bar
So sodden and frayed
I would have titled it "pain-abstract".

I searched your vacant eyes and
My own reflection, was the reason
I did not need to speak nor
Fumble with your beauty

I sipped the thin wine
And watched the moisture
Gather upon your cheeks in
Anticipatory bliss

In that curious instance
Unscathed by broken cliché
And within the contagion of silence
We disappeared together

To run, in haunted lust
Onto the sidewalk now flooded
By the recently busted hydrant
Glowing red in the sun

I thought your legs were endless
Your taste, sublime
Sometimes, the ambiguity of paradise
Can bear striking resemblance to

Room 202

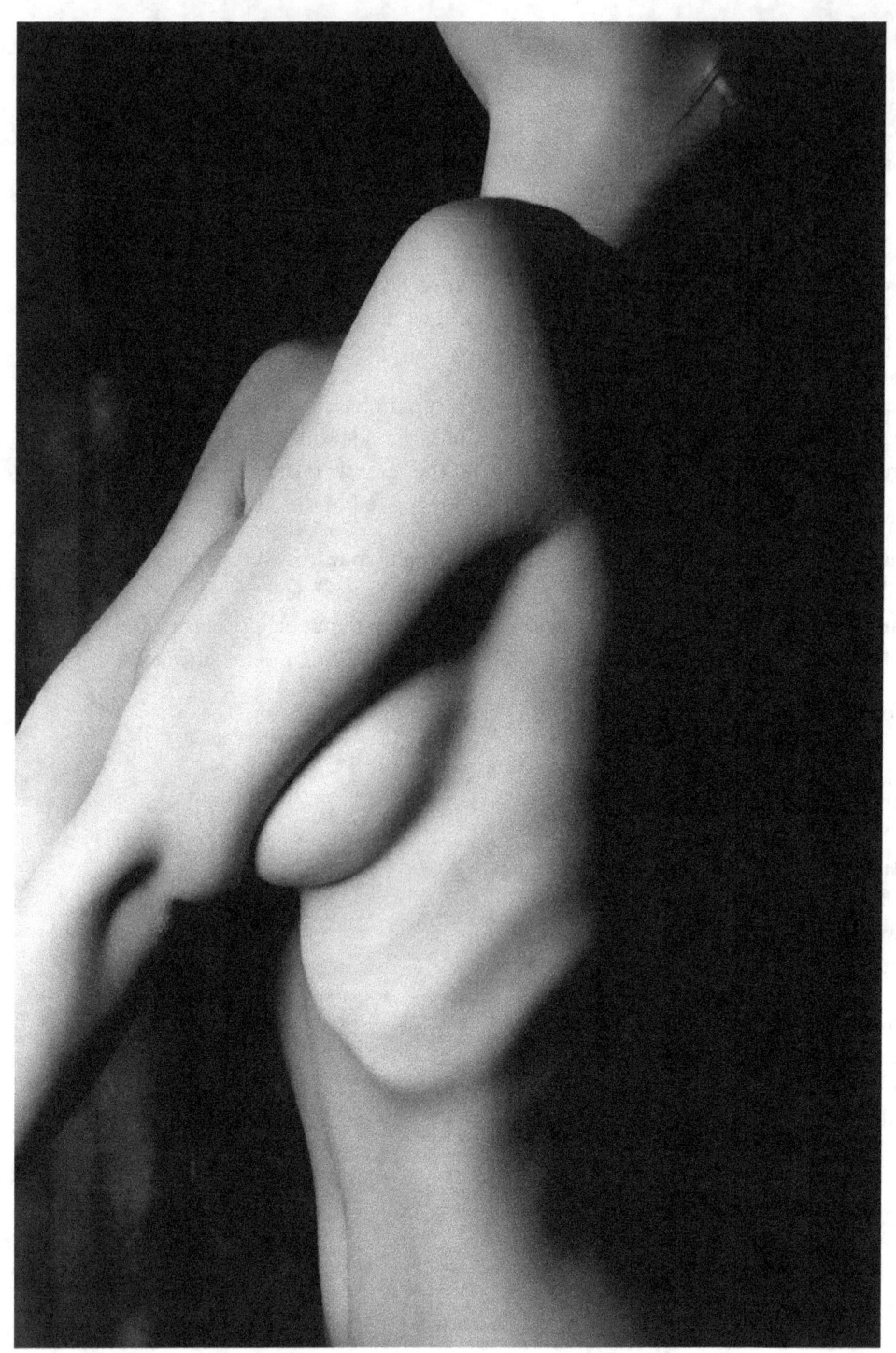

I will wander kindly
Beneath your sky
In hemorrhage asylum
Tasting the scattered
Voices carried upon
The heels of floating paper

I will stand estranged
From mother night
She has abandoned her
Ragged orphan
To the surrogate whores
Of the city

When the air burns heavy
I can feel myself dying
And stare into the windows
At the twisted fragments
Of your acid couplings

To the stockinged beauties
Whose boredom is an art form
I view your galleried sufferings
With vacant companions
In successive encounters

And say that

I will take the
Sweat of
Summer girls
Sweet
Like wine
Upon my tongue

And watch in isolation
This ritual
Searing of the earth

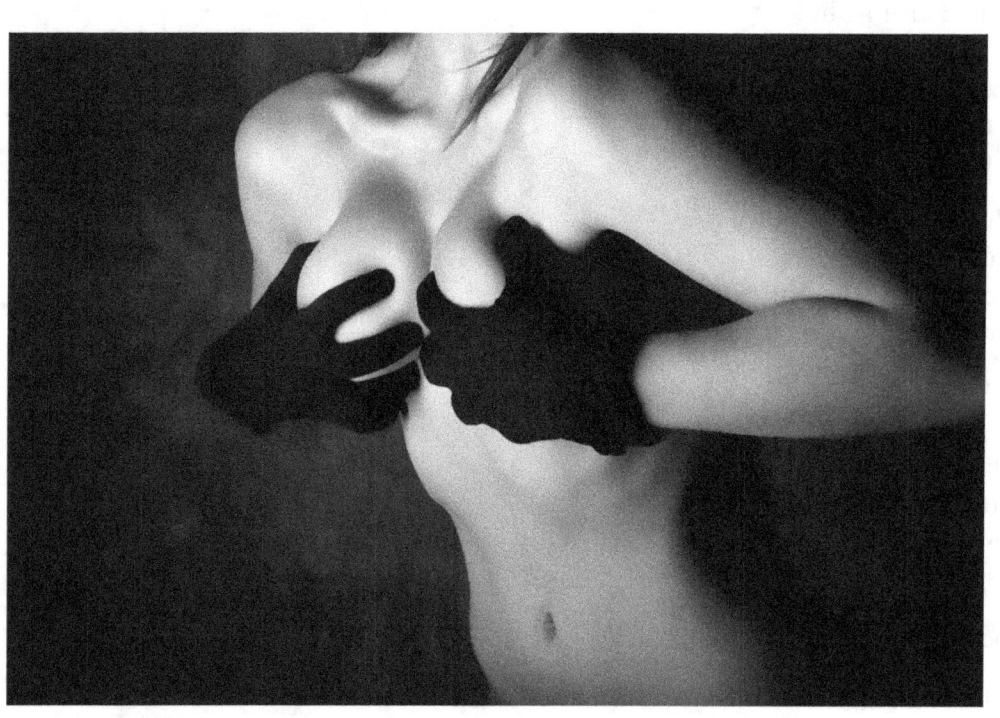

With bitter scorn for death

The sun touched its fingers

Upon your shoulders, and

I glanced the shadow of your breasts

The canvas of silhouette

Painted softly on the wall

As your clothes fell sweetly

Like leaves, to the floor

And you waltzed with sensuality

In the darkness of the room

Your arms laced upon your chest

A playful hesitancy

Tonight, your body

As you lie still

Is not my acquaintance

But holds me in sovereignty

Tonight I will sip the naked skin

Reticently swathed

In your black gloved hands

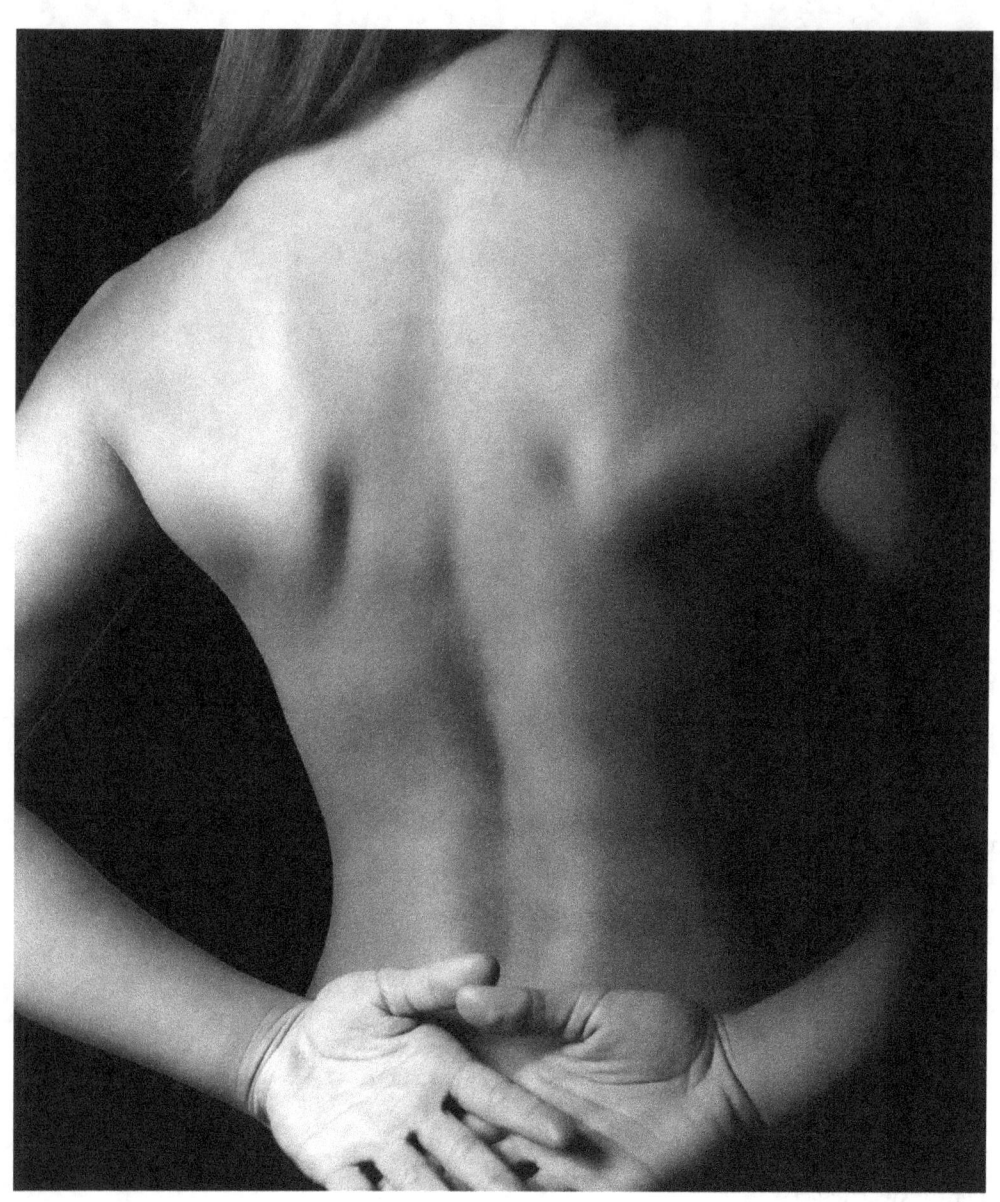

As you have not called
May I say that
I don't care but
Please note that
I don't care about
Much of anything
These days

Kind of blue on
The turntable I bought
For five dollars
From a man on Redpath Ave.
He knew the truth

Miles and I
Tonight will watch
The lights go
On and off
Off and on
In the building
'cross the street.

We'll pretend that
There's a lady waiting
Just for us
In her shadowed apartment
'320-A'

And If I weren't out of cigarettes
We'd smoke
Too

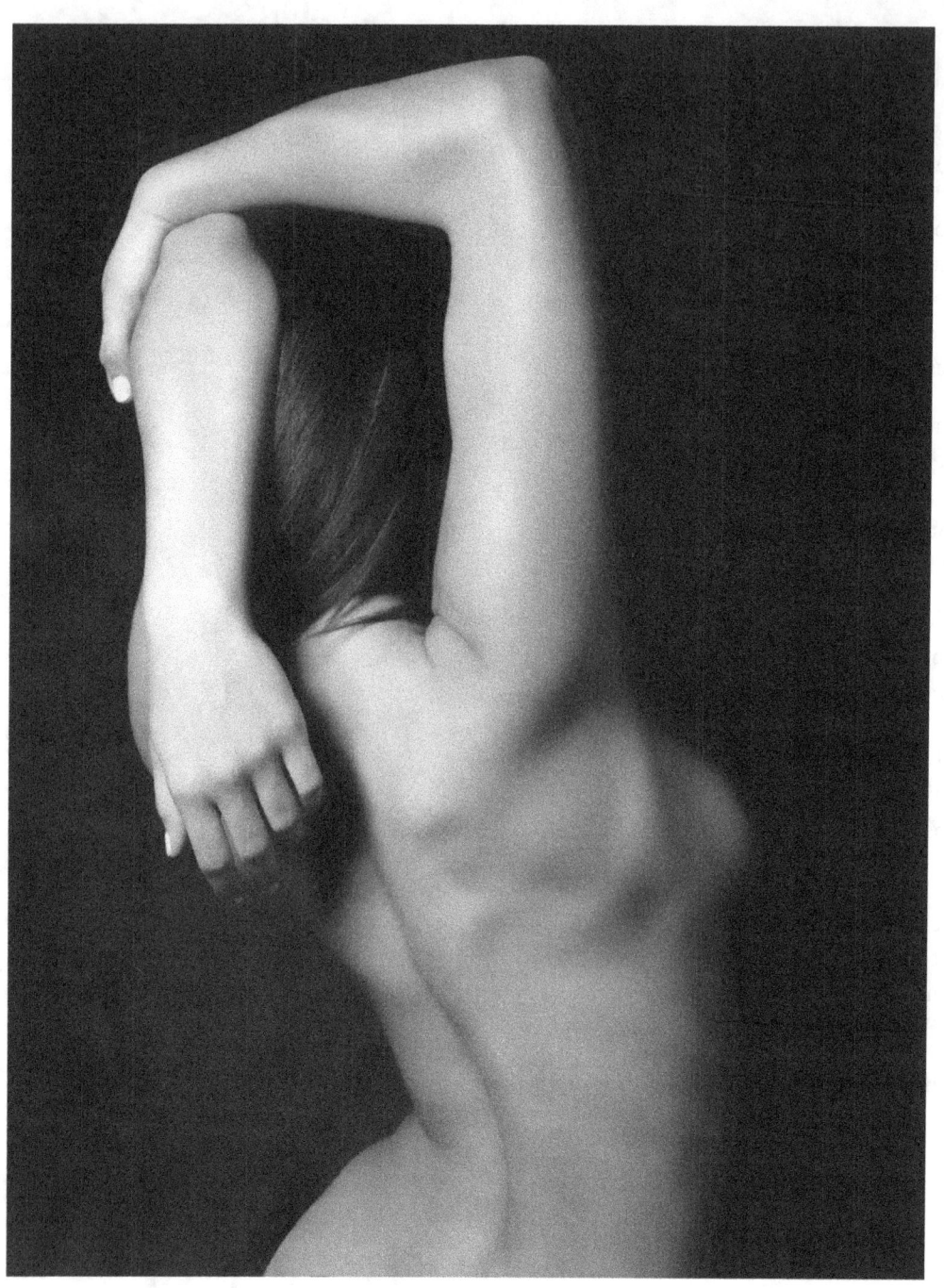

Trees
Dance in the coils of wind
Like me, they are dying
The first breaths of autumn
Grasp them
In executioner's embrace

The late bus
Screams along the boulevard
It conquers the straying dust
Sending it scattered and confused
And leaving me alone
With the night

An old man
Hunched in tragedy
Speaks to me from the shadows
"Son, you got a smoke"?
I look into his mortal eyes
"Yeah, sure"

The cigarette
Rolls within his scarred fingers
"God bless you" he says
"He doesn't" I reply
As he shuffles into the darkness
Looking like he feels sorry for me

The CASH-MONEY sign
Blinks its jaundiced neon
Tonight it is understudy for the absent Moon
She is ensconced with her lover
And abandons me
To the beginning snowfall

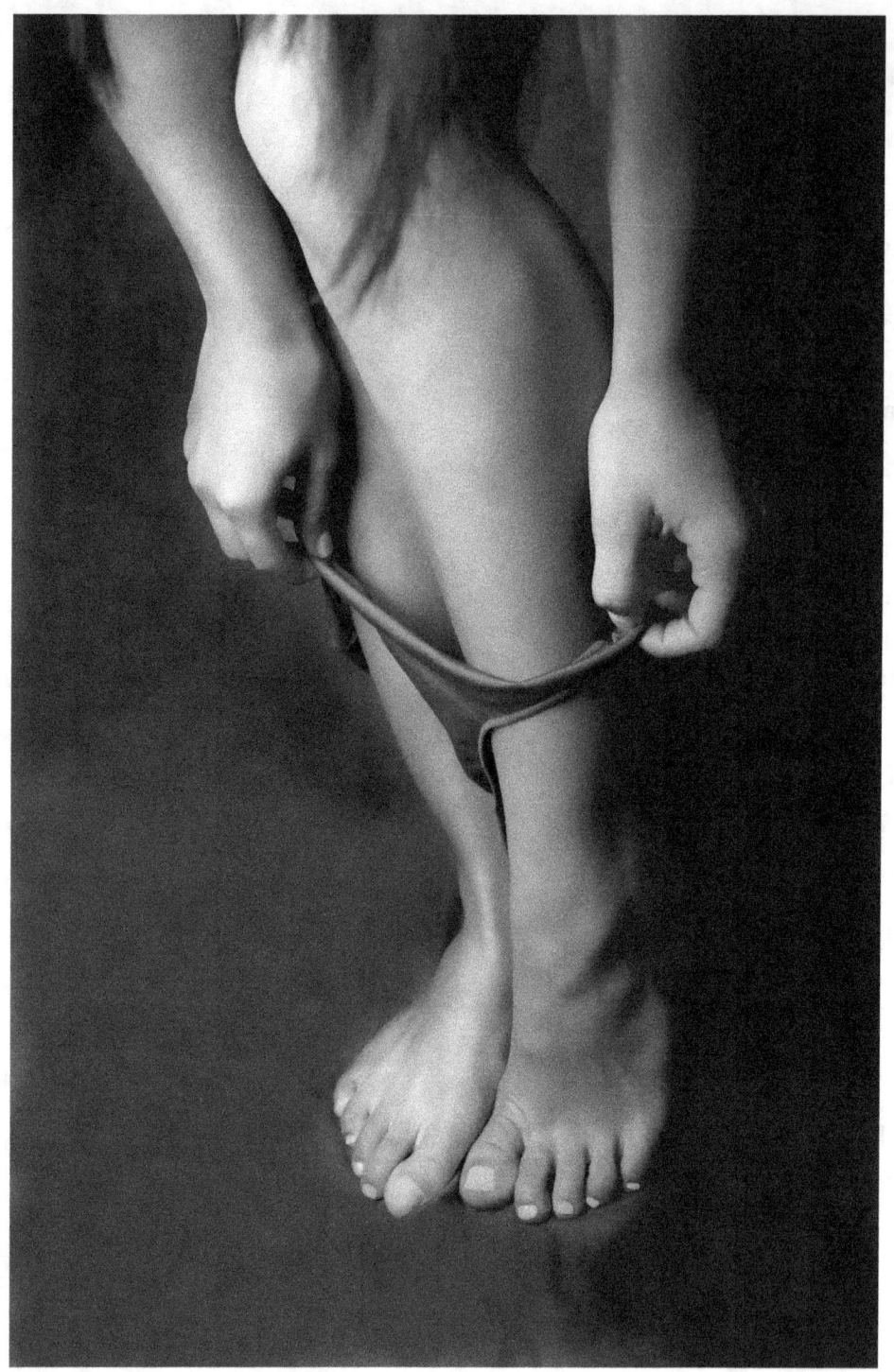

Beside the burning ruins of endless night
Feminine beauty, crimson
Hovers before
My Desiring tongue

The mourned frailty of moments
In the waking silence
Are broken
With wild sensation

As sweet embers drift
From the soul of your flesh
To singe upon my lips
Now trembling with thirst

Acknowledgements

Rhian Owen – Model
Aya Hikone – Hair & Makeup
Henna MacMaster – Photographer Assistant
Truc Chau – Promotional & Marketing Consultant

Please Visit
www.froznmotion.com

www.ingramcontent.com/pod-product-compliance
Lightning Source LLC
Chambersburg PA
CBHW081216170526
45165CB00009B/2843

* 9 7 8 1 4 6 2 0 0 9 7 6 3 *